Cooking USA

50 Favorite Recipes from Across America

GEORGIA ORCUTT

JOHN MARGOLIES

CHRONICLE BOOKS

SAN FRANCISCO

LOOK INSIDE *for beautiful "picture"* map of the entire United States reproduced for you in brilliant colors!

As a special feature of "Travel America Year" The Pullman Company, in association with America's railroads, announces:

Greatest Travel Bargain in History!

LOOK INSIDE ⇨

Library of Congress Cataloging-in-Publication Data:

Orcutt, Georgia.
   Cooking USA : 50 favorite recipes from across America / by Georgia Orcutt and John Margolies.
      p. cm.
   ISBN 0-8118-3960-5 (hardcover)
   1. Cookery, American. I. Margolies, John. II. Title.
   TX715.O59 2004
   641.5973—dc21

2003008939

Manufactured in Singapore.

Designed by Margo Mooney, www.pinkdesigninc.com

Distributed in Canada by Raincoast Books
9050 Shaughnessy Street
Vancouver, British Columbia V6P 6E5

10 9 8 7 6 5 4 3 2 1

Chronicle Books LLC
85 Second Street
San Francisco, California 94105

www.chroniclebooks.com

(Arsenal of Democracy) U. S. A.

UNITY   SECURITY   ALLEGIANCE

COPYRIGHT, 1942, FRANK T. PERONE

DEDICATION

To Stephen, Eli, and Amos, who have enthusiastically tasted the possibilities along all the roads, and to John, who invited me up to see his collection. —*Georgia Orcutt*

ACKNOWLEDGMENTS

We'd like to thank the following people for helping us make this book happen: Margo Mooney at Pink Design, Inc. for her unflagging enthusiasm and design talent; Amy Treadwell, Vivien Sung, and Holly Burrows at Chronicle for graciously steering the project through completion; our agents Jim Fitzgerald and Wendy Burton Brouws for their encouragement; Hy Mariampolski for lending us images from his New York City postcard collection; Molly MacPherson, Susan Kendall, Dan Cherrington, and Patricia Mitchell for contributing opinions on recipes; and Jane Doerfer for lending support at every turn.

GREYHOUND Lines
SCENIC LOW-COST TRAVEL
TO ALL AMERICA

★ IN AMERICA ★
TRAVEL EVERYWHERE BY
GREYHOUND Lines

GREYHOUND LINES

Greyhound Terminals in New York City

Capitol Greyhound Bus Terminal
50th Street and 8th Ave., New York City
Pennsylvania Greyhound Bus Terminal
242 West 34th Street, New York City

49, LEADENHALL STREET, LONDON, E.C. 3.
A. B. REYNOLDSON, General European Agent.

Contents

INTRODUCTION

Wonderful Places to Be—and to Eat

Fifty states. Fifty recipes. Appetizers, drinks, breads, sandwiches, seafood, meat, chicken, desserts. Come with us on a sentimental food journey through the United States and enter a world where you can't buy the same cheesecake in Biloxi as you can in Brooklyn. The trip won't take too long. Each state passes by in the blink of just one classic recipe. On this journey, it's the 1950s or earlier, and although there aren't many chain restaurants to be found on the horizon, mom-and-pops reign supreme, each serving up their own version of home cookin'.

The road beckons, and simply crossing a state line feels like an adventure. From Maine to Montana, from Alabama to California, you'll always know where you are and what state you're in, because residents are proud of their hometowns and they show it. Places promote themselves by the enticing graphics of roadside signs, come-hither travel brochures, catchy postcards, and colorful matchbooks. They're glad to see you, and after all, wherever it is, it's a wonderful place to be.

When it comes to cooking, each state has its own enjoyable way of doing things. Your chowder in Massachusetts will never contain a tomato, and your chili in Texas won't bear a single bean. In Illinois your pizza comes in a mighty deep dish, and in Oklahoma, one bite of your Chicken-Fried Steak is bliss.

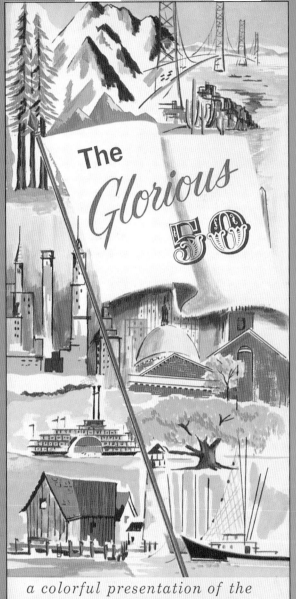

The
Glorious
50

a colorful presentation of the
fascinating stories behind our
FIFTY STATE FLAGS

Bourrillon

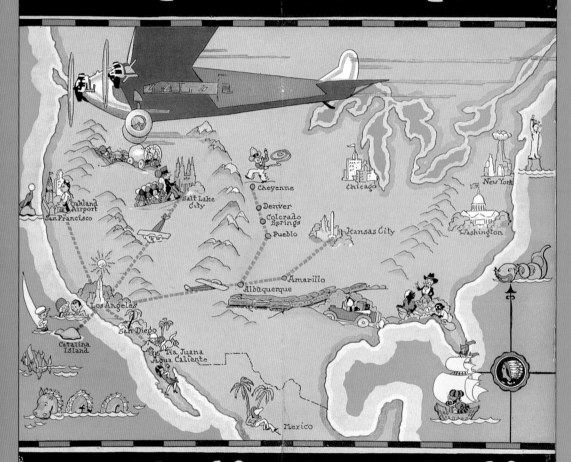

There are an endless number of places to go and something special to savor in every season. In very early spring, crunch some maple sugar atop a bowl of snow in Vermont. Then head to West Virginia in April for a ramp festival to celebrate the tonic effects of wild leeks. (You'll soon understand why everyone there is affectionately called a "little stinker.") In early May, stop in Louisville to watch the Kentucky Derby and discover just the right way to brew a mint julep. Summertime is pie time, and you'll find plenty of slices in Michigan when the cherries are ripe, or in Oregon when the blackberries are harvested. Come fall, head to New Hampshire for apple crisp. And when the weather turns cold up North, head down to the sunny South, stopping in South Carolina for some pulled pork. Or linger in Florida and sample Key lime pie, which absolutely everyone serves. If your journey takes you to the Southwest, discover how chicken is cooked in Santa Fe, or how rice is spiced in Arizona.

Wherever you may travel in these pages, you'll find food with regional character and charm. Eat, drink, and keep right on going. There's another roadside meal around the next bend, and another recipe waiting for you at the next stop. And when you come to the very last page, beat a path to the kitchen and start cooking. There's no time like the present to savor the legendary flavors of every state.

Dinner is Served

1935

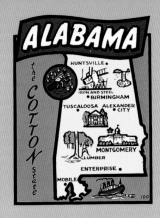

BANANA PUDDING

This homey dessert, which has appeared on menus since the 1930s, still turns up in truck stops and roadside restaurants from Birmingham to Biloxi. It is economical—as it makes use of both egg yolks and whites as well as ripe bananas, which many of us have in excess. Serve warm or cold.

Lay out 16 of the vanilla wafers in a single layer over the bottom of a 9-inch pie dish. Top with a single layer of sliced bananas. Combine the sugar, salt, flour, egg yolks, and vanilla in a mixing bowl and beat with a whisk until smooth. Heat the milk in a medium saucepan over low heat until very warm, but not boiling, about 4 minutes. Pour about 1/2 cup of hot milk into the sugar and egg mixture, whisk until smooth, and pour

32	vanilla wafers (about 1/2 of an 11-ounce box)
3	medium ripe bananas, peeled and thinly sliced
3/4	cup sugar
1/4	teaspoon salt
1/3	cup all-purpose flour
4	egg yolks
1	teaspoon vanilla extract
2	cups whole milk

Topping

4	egg whites
5	tablespoons sugar
1/2	teaspoon vanilla extract

it all back into the saucepan of hot milk. Cook over low heat, whisking frequently, until thick enough for the whisk to leave a mark in the pudding, about 5 minutes. Pour the mixture over the wafer-and-banana layer in the pie dish. Arrange the remaining 16 wafers on edge around the sides of the dish. Let cool slightly.

Make the Topping: Heat the oven to 375 degrees F. Combine the egg whites, sugar, and vanilla in a mixing bowl and beat until stiff peaks form. Spread on top of the pudding and bake for 10 to 12 minutes, or until golden brown. Serve slightly warm or cold.

SERVES 6 TO 8

SALMON PATTIES

Salmon fishing has a long history in Alaska; since 1878, the state has kept a record of its annual pink salmon catch. A nutritious fish, salmon is rich in omega-3 fatty acids and calcium. Pink salmon thrives along the coast of Alaska up into the Bering Sea and is most frequently sold canned. This popular recipe makes short work of dinner using a common Northern pantry staple. Serve these patties on sesame-seed buns and you can call them "salmon burgers."

Heat 1 tablespoon of the oil in a small frying pan and sauté the onion over medium heat, stirring occasionally, until soft, about 5 minutes. Meanwhile, in a medium bowl mix the salmon, eggs, and cracker crumbs together. Add the sautéed onion and season to taste with salt and pepper. Mix well with your hands, and then

4	tablespoons oil
1	medium onion, diced
1	can (17 ounces) salmon, drained, or 2 cups flaked leftover cooked salmon
2	eggs
1	cup crushed cracker crumbs
	Salt and freshly ground black pepper

shape the mixture into 6 hamburger-sized patties, about 3 inches in diameter. Heat the remaining 3 tablespoons of oil in a large frying pan over medium heat and cook the patties for about 5 minutes, or until brown. Turn and cook on the opposite side until brown, about 5 minutes. Serve immediately.

SERVES 4 TO 6

16

ALASKA *tours*

ROBERT
L E E

1935   American Express Travel Service   1935

RED RICE

Cooking and flavors from nearby Mexico are intricately woven into Arizona's cuisine, especially in its southernmost regions. This traditional favorite is often made by ranch cooks, who also add dried chili peppers and corn, which you can stir into the mix for additional flavor. Serve with cornbread.

Heat the oil in a medium saucepan over medium heat, add the onion and garlic, and sauté until soft, about 5 minutes. Add the rice and cook for several minutes, stirring constantly, until the grains are slightly opaque. Add the tomatoes and stock, bring just to a boil, reduce the heat, cover, and simmer for 15 to 20 minutes, or until the rice is just barely dry. Season to taste with salt. Serve hot.

2	tablespoons vegetable oil or bacon drippings
1	medium onion, minced
3	garlic cloves, minced
1	cup uncooked long-grain rice
1	can (8 ounces) diced tomatoes, drained
2	cups chicken stock
	Salt

SERVES 4 TO 6

1939 ARIZONA ROAD MAP

IN COMMEMORATION OF FRAY MARCOS DE NIZA WHO PASSED THIS WAY IN 1539

HIWAY CAFE. BOWIE. ARIZ.

SPECIALIZING IN CHICKEN IN THE ROUGH

LOCKWOOD Cafe

STEAKS   CHOPS   CHICKEN IN THE ROUGH

LOCKWOOD CAFE
HIGHWAY 66 — KINGMAN, ARIZONA

GRAND CANYON

ARIZONA

HUSH PUPPIES

An old Southern favorite to serve with fish, chicken, ham, or pork, these fried cakes taste best served piping hot. Old-timers insist bacon grease is a necessary ingredient, but vegetable oil imparts plenty of flavor, too. You can make the batter a day or two in advance and refrigerate it; let it reach room temperature before cooking.

Combine the eggs, buttermilk, and oil in a mixing bowl and beat with a whisk until smooth. In a separate bowl combine the salt, cornmeal, flour, pepper, baking powder, and baking soda and stir together with a whisk. Add the egg mixture to the dry ingredients and stir just until blended. Set aside.

2	eggs
1	cup buttermilk
2	tablespoons vegetable oil or bacon grease
1/2	teaspoon salt
2	cups yellow cornmeal
1	cup all-purpose flour
1/4	teaspoon freshly ground black pepper
1	teaspoon baking powder
1/2	teaspoon baking soda
	Cooking oil for frying

Bluff Cafe, Mountainburg, Ark.

ARKANSAS

Jes' doin' what comes naturally

Add the cooking oil to a deep-fat fryer and set it on medium-high, or heat 2 inches of oil in a large kettle until a small drop of batter sizzles on contact. When the oil is hot, drop the batter in by tablespoonfuls and cook, turning as necessary to brown evenly, for approximately 4 minutes, or until brown on all sides. When done they should float to the surface. Drain on paper towels. Serve hot.

SERVES 6 TO 8; MAKES ABOUT 10

THE TOWERS

TOWERS

FRIED CHICKEN TOWERS CAFE K·C STEAKS

TEXARKANA, U.S.A.   OB-H541

GUACAMOLE

The California avocado industry began in the late 1920s with the cultivation of the Hass avocado, named after postman Rudolph Hass, who discovered the tree in his La Habra backyard. The piquant dip has been synonymous with the state ever since.

Halve the avocados and remove the pits. Scoop the pulp into a bowl. Drizzle it with lemon juice and mash well with a fork. Add the salt, cilantro, onion, and tomato and mix well. Serve with corn chips for dipping.

SERVES 8 TO 10

2	ripe avocados, preferably Hass
3	tablespoons fresh lemon or lime juice
1/2	teaspoon salt
2	tablespoons minced fresh cilantro
1/2	cup diced onion
3	tablespoons chopped tomato

DENVER OMELET

The origin of this popular dish remains a mystery, but it has been known around Colorado's capital city and beyond for decades. A favorite for a truly hearty Western-style breakfast, this oven-baked omelet is also eaten for dinner. To make it even richer, use half-and-half instead of milk.

Heat the oven to 400 degrees F. Grease a 10-inch round baking dish (or make the entire recipe in a cast-iron skillet). Melt the butter in a skillet over medium-low heat. Add the onion and bell pepper and cook for about 5 minutes, stirring occasionally, until soft. Add the ham and cook for 2 minutes more. Remove from the heat. Beat the eggs and milk in a large bowl. Stir in the cheese and add the sautéed vegetables and ham. Season to taste with salt and pepper. Transfer the mixture to the prepared dish.

2	tablespoons butter
1	medium onion, chopped
1	green or red bell pepper, seeded and chopped
1	cup chopped cooked ham
8	eggs
1/4	cup milk
1	cup (4 ounces) grated cheddar cheese
	Salt and freshly ground black pepper

(If baking in a cast-iron skillet, pour egg mixture with cheese over the vegetables and ham.) Bake for 20 minutes or until the top is puffy and brown. Cut into wedges and serve warm.

SERVES 4 TO 6

COLORADO STATE FAIR PUEBLO AUG. 28 SEPT. 1 HOWDY!

PULLING LEATHER

SEE COLORADO THE SCENIC STATE

Famous Chef Restaurant
On Highway 40 & 36

Famous CHEF

Famous CHEF

From a Sandwich to a Complete Meal

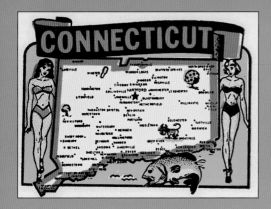

BAKED SHAD

Connecticut River shad are born in freshwater, spend three or more years in saltwater, and then return to freshwater to mate. In search of a spawning ground, many travel up the Connecticut River. They are expected when the forsythia blooms, and freshly caught, have been cause for culinary celebration for more than a century. The fish, which range in size from about 2 to 5 pounds, each yield two fillets, or "sides." Allow approximately 1/2 pound per person. Serve with fresh asparagus and new potatoes.

2	pounds shad fillets
2	tablespoons butter
1/4	cup white wine
4	lemon wedges

Heat the oven to 350 degrees F. Arrange the shad fillets in a greased baking dish. Cut the butter into small dollops and dot evenly over the fish. Sprinkle each fillet with some of the wine. Bake for 5 minutes per 1/2-inch of thickness, just until the fish flakes easily. Garnish each plate with a lemon wedge and serve immediately.

SERVES 4

CONNECTICUT
invites you to its
TERCENTENARY

1635 1935

QUI TRANSTULIT SUSTINET

Communication 300 years ago

and to enjoy its unsurpassed playgrounds amid historic surroundings

CONNECTICUT

PUTNAM

TORRINGTON

★ HARTFORD

WATERBURY

NORWICH

MIDDLETOWN

DANBURY

DERBY

106

THE *Constitution* STATE

CASINO GRILL

CASINO

CASINO GRILL

SAYBROOK, CONN.

BOSTON POST ROAD — *Phone 329* —

DELAWARE

WILMINGTON
NEWARK

DOVER

FORT
SALISBURY

REHOBOTH
BEACH

GEORGETOWN

Blue Hen State

The First State

BAKED CHICKEN

This recipe is a legacy of Delaware's Chicken-of-Tomorrow Contest, launched in 1948 by fryer chicken producers on the Delmarva Peninsula. At its inception, the event featured the world's largest frying pan (ten feet in diameter), made in Selbyville and capable of cooking eight hundred chicken quarters at once. Not by happenstance, the Blue Hen chicken, a ferocious fighter, is the official state bird. Serve with steamed rice and a tossed salad.

1/2	cup bottled Italian dressing
1	broiler-fryer chicken (about 2 pounds), cut in parts and skinned
1	cup Italian seasoned bread crumbs
1/2	teaspoon salt
1/4	teaspoon paprika
1	tablespoon butter, melted

Pour the dressing into a shallow, nonmetallic container. Add the chicken and turn to coat on all sides. Cover with plastic wrap and marinate in the refrigerator for a minimum of 30 minutes and up to 24 hours. When ready to bake, heat the oven to 375 degrees F. Combine the bread crumbs, salt, and paprika in a shallow bowl. Remove the chicken from the marinade, draining off excess dressing. Place the chicken pieces in the crumb mixture, turning to coat on all sides. Arrange the chicken pieces in a foil-lined baking pan and drizzle the melted butter over them. Bake for 50 minutes or until the chicken is brown and fork tender.

SERVES 4

The Sunshine State

KEY LIME PIE

Key lime pie comes from the Florida Keys and predates the arrival of fresh milk and electricity to the islands. The real thing needs tiny, juicy, and flavorful greenish yellow Key limes, but you can cheat and use bigger supermarket limes with fine results. Although the pie will set without chilling if you use the highly acidic Key lime juice, it's a good idea to bake the pie for a short time to eliminate the possibility of salmonella bacteria in the uncooked egg yolks.

Heat the oven to 350 degrees F. Grease a 9-inch pie pan. To make the crust: Place the graham crackers in a heavy-duty plastic bag and crush with a rolling pin, or crumble them into a food processor and pulse until ground into fine crumbs. Place the crumbs in a mixing bowl and drizzle with the melted butter. Stir with a fork until evenly damp.

Crust

10	whole graham crackers
6	tablespoons butter, melted

Filling

3	egg yolks
2	teaspoons grated lime zest
1	can (14 ounces) sweetened condensed milk
2/3	cup freshly squeezed lime juice (about 12 Key limes or 4 supermarket limes)

Whipped cream for garnish

Press the mixture into the bottom and sides of the prepared pie pan. Bake for 6 minutes, until slightly brown and firm. Set aside to cool.

To make the filling: Combine the egg yolks and lime zest and beat with an electric mixer on medium speed for several minutes until smooth. Add the condensed milk and continue to beat for 4 minutes, until the mixture thickens. Reduce the mixer speed and trickle in the lime juice, beating just until smooth. Pour the mixture into the prebaked pie shell and bake for 12 minutes, or until the filling is set and doesn't jiggle. Cool on a rack and then chill for at least 2 hours. Freeze for 30 minutes before serving. The pie can also be wrapped with plastic wrap and frozen whole; let it sit at room temperature for about 20 minutes before serving. Garnish each serving generously with whipped cream.

SERVES 6 TO 8

GEORGIA *Peach*
R034

PEACH CAKE

In the late 1800s, Elberta peaches put Georgia on the map. Today, commercial growers tend more than forty different varieties. This cake is a popular and easy way to use fresh peaches. Absolutely any variety will do, but be sure every peach you use is dead ripe— if it is perfectly ripe it will feel like a mule's nose, just slightly soft.

Heat the oven to 375 degrees F. Grease an 8-inch square baking pan. Peel and pit the peaches and cut into thin slices. Put the slices in a medium saucepan with the 1/4 cup sugar and the lemon juice. Stir gently and cook over low heat for 5 minutes, until the juice in the pan starts to boil. Spoon the mixture into the prepared pan and set aside.

4	medium ripe peaches (about 1 pound)
1/4	cup sugar
	Juice from 1/2 lemon

Topping

1/2	cup all-purpose flour
1/2	cup packed brown sugar
1/2	teaspoon ground cinnamon
1/4	teaspoon salt
4	tablespoons (1/2 stick) cold butter

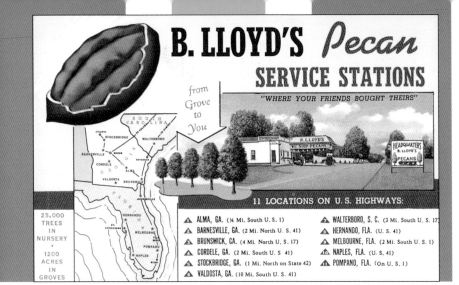

Cake

- 1/4 **teaspoon baking soda**
- 1/2 **teaspoon baking powder**
- 3/4 **cup all-purpose flour**
- 1/4 **teaspoon salt**
- 4 **tablespoons (1/2 stick) unsalted butter, softened**
- 1/4 **cup sugar**
- 1 **teaspoon vanilla extract**
- 1/2 **cup sour cream**
- 1 **egg**

To make the topping: Combine the flour, brown sugar, cinnamon, and salt in a food processor and pulse until blended. Cut the butter into small pieces, add to the mixture, and pulse just until coarse crumbs form. Set aside.

To make the cake: Combine the baking soda, baking powder, flour, and salt in a mixing bowl and blend with a whisk. Set aside. Combine the butter and sugar in a mixing bowl and beat well. Add the vanilla, sour cream, and egg and beat until blended. Gradually add the flour mixture and beat just until the batter is smooth. Spoon the batter on top of the peaches, smoothing it with a spatula until all the fruit is covered. Sprinkle the crumb topping over the batter. Bake for 20 to 25 minutes, until a toothpick inserted in the center comes out clean.

SERVES 6 TO 8

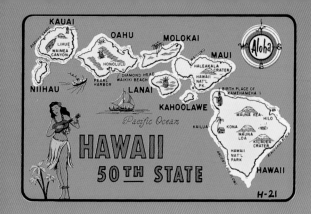

SWEET-AND-SOUR SPARERIBS

In the mid-nineteenth century, Hawaii's sugar industry imported workers from China, Japan, Korea, Portugal, the Philippines, Polynesia, and Puerto Rico, and local food traditions have long reflected the diversity of these cultures. In 1903, a special tourism committee was created to promote the new Territory to the world; this recipe represents the ethnically diverse "Island Cooking" that has enticed travelers for more than one hundred years. Serve these tangy ribs with steamed rice and pickled vegetables.

2	pounds pork spareribs
1	tablespoon soy sauce
2	tablespoons all-purpose flour
3	tablespoons vegetable oil
1	clove garlic, crushed
1	1½-inch piece fresh ginger root, peeled and crushed
2/3	cup cider vinegar
1½	cups water
1	cup packed brown sugar
2	teaspoons salt

Ask the butcher to cut the spareribs crosswise into 1 1/2-inch-long pieces. Place the ribs in a large shallow glass or stainless-steel pan. Sprinkle the soy sauce and flour over the ribs, mixing gently. Heat the oil in a large saucepan. Add the ribs, garlic, and ginger and brown the ribs over medium heat for 5 to 6 minutes, turning once to cook evenly. Drain off the fat. Add the vinegar, water, brown sugar, and salt and simmer for 45 minutes over medium-low heat, until the meat is tender. Serve hot.

SERVES 6

HAWAII

· Duke Kahanamoku ·
World's Champion Swimmer
"On The Beach at Waikiki"

SPUD

IDAHO

The Gem State

BAKED STUFFED POTATOES

Pioneers first grew potatoes in Idaho in the 1860s, and by 1912 the University of Idaho established its first agricultural experiment station at Aberdeen, to study them as a commercial crop. For potatoes to earn the status of being called "Idaho," they must be grown in the state. The most popular commercial varieties, which include Russett Burbank, are oblong, with dark brown netted skin, perfect for baking. Never, ever bake them in aluminum foil, which steams the flesh (although it's okay to wrap them in foil after they're baked to keep them warm).

3	large Idaho potatoes (approximately 9 ounces each)
1	small onion, diced
2	teaspoons olive oil
1	cup sour cream
	Salt and freshly ground black pepper

Heat the oven to 400 degrees F. Scrub the potatoes and prick in several places with a fork. Bake for approximately 1 hour, or until soft throughout. Remove the potatoes and reduce the oven heat to 350 degrees F. Using an oven mitt to hold them, slice each potato in half

lengthwise and gently scoop out the pulp into a large bowl, leaving a thin layer of potato flesh next to the skin all around. Work carefully to keep the skins intact, placing them in a shallow baking dish after you remove the pulp.

Sauté the onion in the olive oil in a medium skillet over medium heat for 2 to 3 minutes, until soft. Add to the potato pulp along with the sour cream and mix well with a big spoon. Season to taste with salt and pepper. Spoon the potato mixture into the potato skins, dividing equally, and bake for 10 to 15 minutes, until hot. Serve immediately.

SERVES 6

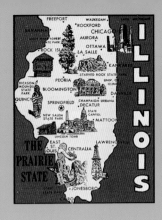

CHICAGO PIZZA

According to pizza legend, Ike Seawell created the first deep-dish–style Chicago pizza in 1943, and several decades later it was put on the United States map by the Pizzeria Uno chain. The secret to deep-dish pizza is the crust; this recipe, which uses packaged pizza dough, will give you a tasty approximation of the real thing in short order. For variations, add chopped onions, pepperoni, sliced mushrooms, or Italian sausage before adding the Parmesan cheese.

2	packages (1 pound each) refrigerated pizza dough
1/2	pound sliced mozzarella cheese
2	cans (28 ounces each) Italian-style whole tomatoes, drained
2	teaspoons dried oregano
1/2	cup grated Parmesan cheese
2	tablespoons olive oil

Heat the oven to 450 degrees F. Oil a deep-dish pizza pan (approximately 14 inches in diameter). Remove the dough from the packages and press it together to form 1 large ball. Flatten the ball into a disk, place it in the oiled pan, and press it with your fingertips to evenly cover the bottom and come up the sides of the pan to a thickness of about 1/8 inch. Arrange slices of mozzarella evenly on the bottom of the crust-lined pan. With your hands, squeeze the tomatoes over a strainer, breaking them up into pieces, and then scatter over the mozzarella. Sprinkle with oregano and top with Parmesan cheese. Drizzle the olive oil over the top. Bake for 30 minutes or until the top is golden and the crust is lightly browned.

SERVES 6 TO 8

The Hoosier State

HOOSIER MEAT LOAF

Menus from diners and mom-and-pop restaurants throughout Indiana have featured moist, tasty meat loaf since the 1940s. It's easy to make and fancy enough for company; a popular Indianapolis caterer currently offers it as a buffet item for corporate events.

Heat the oven to 350 degrees F. Combine all of the ingredients in a large bowl and mix well with clean hands. Pat the mixture into a 9-by-5-inch loaf pan and bake for 1 hour, 15 minutes, or until a meat thermometer inserted in the center reads 160 degrees F. Remove from the oven and let cool slightly. Drain off excess fat before slicing and serving.

SERVES 8 TO 10

1	pound ground beef
1	pound ground pork
1 1/2	cups rolled oats
2	eggs, beaten
1	teaspoon ground allspice
1/2	teaspoon dried thyme
1	medium onion, minced
1	green bell pepper, seeded and minced
	Salt and freshly ground pepper

Hawthorn Restaurant, Inc.
Indianapolis, Ind.

BOXMAN'S
RESTAURANT
Since 1928

GUEST of Indiana Hoosierland

CORN CASSEROLE

Iowa is the nation's number one corn producer, and has held this title for decades. Many residents can still sing "The Iowa Corn Song," which dates to 1912. This easy side dish is a local favorite in the land of endless fields and working farms.

1	can (17 ounces) creamed corn
1	cup fresh bread crumbs
1	cup milk
1	green bell pepper, seeded and chopped
	Salt and freshly ground black pepper
1/2	pound cheddar cheese, thinly sliced
4	strips bacon, cooked until crisp and crumbled (optional)

Heat the oven to 325 degrees F. Combine the corn, bread crumbs, milk, and bell pepper in a large bowl, and stir to mix well. Season to taste with salt and pepper. Pour the mixture into a greased 1-quart casserole dish. Top with cheese and the bacon, if using. Bake for 1 hour, or until the edges are slightly brown. Serve hot.

SERVES 4 TO 6

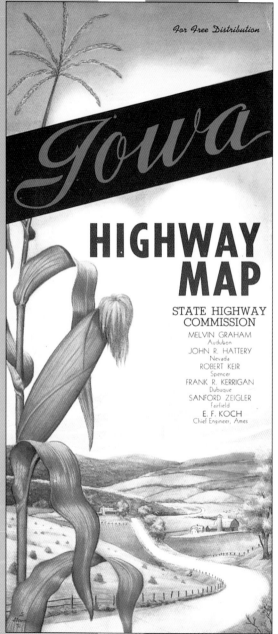

For Free Distribution

Iowa

HIGHWAY MAP

STATE HIGHWAY COMMISSION

MELVIN GRAHAM
Audubon

JOHN R. HATTERY
Nevada

ROBERT KEIR
Spencer

FRANK R. KERRIGAN
Dubuque

SANFORD ZEIGLER
Fairfield

E. F. KOCH
Chief Engineer, Ames

IOWA

CORN-BRED CHARMER

MARSHALL'S
CAFE & DRIVEIN

JUNCTIONS
30 64 & 63

TAMA IOWA

I EAT AT
MARSHALL'S
TAMA

PIONEER BREAD

Kansas earned its second nickname, the Wheat State, decades ago, and it continues to be the largest wheat producer in the country. If you took a year's average crop, it would fill train cars stretching from its western border all the way to the Atlantic Ocean. Not by coincidence, the Home Baking Association, the only nonprofit communications program that still promotes baking at home, is headquartered in Topeka. This tasty bread is typical of the hearty, homemade loaves still served in farm kitchens.

1	package (1/4 ounce) active dry yeast
1/4	cup warm water (110 degrees to 115 degrees F)
1/4	cup yellow cornmeal, plus 2 to 3 tablespoons cornmeal for pans
2	tablespoons packed brown sugar
1	teaspoon salt
2	tablespoons vegetable oil
1/2	cup boiling water
1/2	cup cool water
1/2	cup whole-wheat flour
1/4	cup rye flour
2	to 2 1/4 cups bread flour

Dissolve the yeast in 1/4 cup warm water and let sit for 5 minutes until the mixture is slightly thickened. In a large mixing bowl or bowl of a standing mixer, combine the 1/4 cup cornmeal, brown sugar, salt, and oil with 1/2 cup boiling water. Stir in 1/2 cup cool water. Let sit until lukewarm (110 degrees to 115 degrees F). With a large wooden spoon stir in the dissolved yeast. Beat in the whole-wheat and rye flours, mixing well. Stir in enough of the bread flour to make a soft dough. Knead 10 to 12 minutes by hand on a floured surface or with the mixer's dough hook. Place the dough in a lightly greased bowl, turning to grease the top. Cover with plastic wrap; let rise until doubled, about 1 hour.

Punch the dough down and divide into 2 equal pieces. Cover and let rest 10 minutes. Grease and sprinkle two 9-inch pie plates or a baking sheet with cornmeal. Shape each dough piece into a round loaf and place in the pan(s). Cover with plastic wrap; let rise until doubled, about 1 hour. Heat the oven to 375 degrees F. With a sharp knife slash the top of each loaf in a decorative pattern. Bake 25 to 30 minutes or until the loaves sound hollow when gently tapped. Remove from the pan(s) and cool on wire racks.

MAKES 2 SMALL ROUND LOAVES

MINT JULEPS

It would be impossible to separate this drink from the Kentucky Derby, which dates back to 1875 and is held the first Saturday in May. Special techniques abound for making the beverage. Some bartenders bruise the mint in white handkerchiefs; others insist on superfine sugar or powdered sugar; and some blend the bourbon with the mint to get just the right flavor balance before building a drink. Start the preparations a good day in advance and make sure you have a tall glass in hand by post time: 6:00 P.M. Eastern Standard Time.

10	sprigs fresh mint, plus additional for garnish
2	cups natural spring water
2	cups sugar
	Crushed ice
1	bottle (750 ml) bourbon

LOUISVILLE'S CHOICE FOR STEAKS, CHOPS AND SEA FOOD

STEBBINS GRILL

STEBBINS GRILL   412 W. CHESTNUT STREET   LOUISVILLE 2, KENTUCKY

THE
KENTUCKY CARDINAL
From an original painting by John James Audubon

• HISTORY • SCENERY • ROMANCE •

Wash the mint. Tear some of the leaves, keeping 6 to 8 sprigs whole. Spread the whole sprigs in the bottom of a 1 1/2-quart plastic container. Bring the spring water to a boil in a heavy saucepan and add the sugar. Do not stir. Keep the mixture boiling for 5 minutes. Pour the hot syrup over the mint sprigs, making sure to scrape out any sugar from the bottom of the pan. Sprinkle the remaining torn mint on top. Cover and refrigerate overnight, preferably for at least 12 hours. At serving time, spoon crushed ice into tall glasses and add bourbon and syrup to taste. (Some recipes call for a proportion of half bourbon and half syrup; the sweeter the drink, the easier it is on novices.) Garnish each glass with a mint sprig.

SERVES 10 TO 12

CHICKEN GUMBO

This flavorful stew was made popular by Southern slaves, its name derived from several African words for okra, which was traditionally added as thickening ingredient. Almost all gumbos use filé, a spice made from the dried leaves of the sassafras tree. The dish reflects the traditions of local French, Spanish, Indian, and African cooks in Louisiana, and can contain seafood, chicken, meat, and a wide variety of vegetables. Serve it with hot rice.

1/2	cup olive oil
1/2	cup all-purpose flour
2	medium onions, chopped
1	green bell pepper, seeded and chopped
3	cloves garlic, minced
1	pound smoked sausage, thinly sliced crosswise
2	quarts chicken stock
1/2	teaspoon cayenne pepper
1	teaspoon gumbo filé
3 1/2	cups cubed cooked boneless chicken
	Salt and freshly ground black pepper

Heat the oil in a Dutch oven over low heat. Gradually add the flour and cook over medium-low heat, stirring frequently, until the mixture (called a *roux*) is chocolate brown, about 20 minutes. Add the onions, bell pepper, garlic, and sausage; reduce the heat to low and cook for 10 minutes, stirring frequently, until the *roux* is well incorporated. Add the stock, cayenne, and filé and increase the heat to high. Stir gently until the mixture is just starting to bubble. Add the chicken, reduce the heat to a simmer, and cook for 30 minutes, stirring frequently, until the gumbo is fragrant and hot. Season with salt and pepper to taste.

SERVES 6 TO 8

STEAMED LOBSTER

Lobster has long been *the* symbol of Maine, and for years it has been just about impossible to find a restaurant in the state that doesn't offer the delicious crustacean on the menu—boiled, steamed, broiled, baked, adorning chowder, or folded into a simple roll. Lobster shacks dating back to the 1920s are still popular. Cooks statewide and throughout New England debate the merits of steamed versus boiled lobster. The former produces sweet meat and won't fill your plate with water, and that's the technique used here. Steam for 13 minutes per pound, for the first pound. Add 3 minutes per pound for each additional pound. For example, a 11/2-pound lobster will cook in 141/2 minutes, and a 2 pound lobster in 16 minutes. Serve your perfectly cooked lobster with melted butter, corn on the cob, and hot rolls.

4	whole live lobsters (about 1 1/2 pounds each)

Add 2 inches of seawater or salted water to a pot large enough to comfortably hold the lobsters. (Some cooks also place, in the bottom of the pot, a steaming rack large enough to hold the lobsters above the water. Specially made lobster steaming kettles include this feature.) Bring the water to a rolling boil over high heat. Remove the bands from the lobster claws with

a sharp knife, put the lobsters in the pot, cover tightly, and return to a boil as quickly as possible. Steam for 14 to 16 minutes, depending on the weight of the lobsters.

Note: The cooking time is for hard-shell lobsters; if you're cooking new soft-shell lobsters, reduce the steaming time by 3 minutes overall. When you can easily pull off the antennae and the bodies are bright red, the lobsters are done. Lift them out of the kettle with tongs, put them on large dinner plates or platters, and get to work with lobster crackers and picks.

SERVES 4

CRAB CAKES

In the Chesapeake Bay area, a region synonymous with great seafood, Atlantic blue crabs are still taken to crab houses as they have been for decades, where they are steamed whole and picked clean of meat by workers with flying fingers. A good portion of the catch is served up as crab cakes in local seafood restaurants.

Combine all ingredients except the butter and oil in a mixing bowl and gently toss with a fork just until well mixed. Use your hands to shape the mixture into 8 patties, about 3 inches in diameter and 1/2 inch thick. Heat the butter and oil in a large frying pan over medium heat until just barely sizzling. Add the crab cakes and cook for 5 minutes or until browned. Turn and cook on the other side for another 5 minutes or until brown. Serve hot with lemon wedges and cole slaw.

1	pound fresh crabmeat
1/2	green or red bell pepper, seeded and diced
1/2	onion, diced
3	tablespoons mayonnaise
1	egg
1/2	cup fresh bread crumbs
2	teaspoons Old Bay seasoning
2	teaspoons sherry
	Salt and freshly ground black pepper
1	tablespoon butter
1	tablespoon olive oil

SERVES 4 TO 6

Progressive City in the Heart of MARYLAND

Beautiful and Historic FREDERICK

"The clustered spires of Frederick stand Green-Walled by the hills of Maryland"

Compliments of
The News-Post
Frederick County's
HOME NEWSPAPERS

C.C. DEITESFELD

Copyright News-Post, Frederick, Md.

53

1775

MINUTEMEN MEET THE BRITISH AT LEXINGTON AND CONCORD

MASSACHUSETTS

CLAM CHOWDER

Among the many kinds of chowder, clam reigns supreme in Massachusetts. Herman Melville sang its praises in *Moby Dick*, and Boston-based Legal Seafoods has sent their brand to Washington, D.C., for each presidential inauguration since 1981. You'll find clam chowder by the cup or bowl from Springfield to Provincetown. The real thing is built in layers, never ever contains tomatoes, and always tastes better the next day.

Bring a kettle of water to a boil over high heat. Meanwhile, put the salt pork in a Dutch oven and cook over medium heat until crisp. Scoop out the bits and set aside for a garnish. Leave the fat in the pan. Add the onions and sauté over medium heat until soft, about 5 minutes.

1/4	cup diced salt pork, or 3 strips bacon, diced
2	medium onions, thinly sliced
4	cups peeled, sliced white potatoes (about 1 1/2 pounds)
1/2	cup crushed pilot crackers or Saltines
1	quart freshly shucked clams, minced, with their juice (about 10 pounds unshucked clams; see Note)
4	cups whole milk, half-and-half, or a combination of the two
	Salt and freshly ground black pepper

Remove about half the onions from the pan with a slotted spoon and reserve in a bowl. Scatter a layer of sliced potatoes over the onions remaining in the bottom of the pan, and then add a sprinkling of cracker crumbs. Repeat each layer to use up all the onions, potatoes, and cracker crumbs. Add enough of the boiling water to barely reach the top layer. Cover and cook over medium-low heat until the potatoes are tender, about 30 minutes. Stir in the clams and their juice. Heat the milk in a saucepan over medium-low heat just until it is hot, and add to the chowder. Simmer gently for 5 minutes, just until the clams are heated through. Do not let the chowder boil or the clams will be tough. Season to taste with salt and pepper. Garnish each serving with the reserved crispy salt pork. Serve immediately.

SERVES 8 TO 10

Note: Shucking clams is an art that takes time to perfect. If you don't have time to open each clam, combine 3 cups of water and 1 cup of white wine in a large kettle and bring to a boil. Gently add the clams, cover, and simmer for about 3 or 4 minutes, just until the clam shells open. (Don't overcook or the clams will be rubbery.) Remove the clams with a slotted spoon and pull the meat out of the shells and mince. Strain the stock through cheesecloth and use it and the meat to make the soup.

CHERRY PIE

Michigan's tart cherry industry was well established around Traverse City and along Lake Michigan by the early 1900s, and since 1926 the state has hosted the National Cherry Festival. This pie could easily be considered one of the state's official foods.

2	cans (16 ounces each) unsweetened tart cherries, or 4 cups frozen unsweetened tart cherries, unthawed
1	cup sugar
3	tablespoons quick-cooking tapioca or cornstarch
1/2	teaspoon almond extract
	Unbaked pastry for a 2-crust, 9-inch pie, rolled into two 11-inch rounds
2	tablespoons butter, cut into pieces

Heat the oven to 400 degrees F. If using canned cherries, drain them well. (Discard the juice or save for another use.) Combine the cherries, sugar, tapioca, and almond extract in a large mixing bowl and stir gently to mix well. Let stand for 15 minutes. Line a 9-inch pie plate with 1 pastry round. Fill with the cherry mixture. Dot with the butter. Add the remaining round for the top crust, crimping and trimming the edges as necessary to form a tight pastry seal. Cut slits for steam to escape, or make a lattice-top pie. Bake for 50 to 55 minutes, or until the crust is golden brown and the filling is bubbly. Let the pie cool for at least 1 hour before serving.

SERVES 6 TO 8

BAKED WALLEYE

Minnesota is known for its great fishing. One of the most popular fish is the walleye, a member of the perch family, which originally inhabited the larger lakes and rivers but has been introduced into many more waterways. In the state's best fishing spots, it can grow to 26 inches; the state record is a 17-pound, 8-ounce walleye caught in the Seagull River. Here's one of the most popular ways to cook a catch—of any size. Serve with fried potatoes and a green salad.

Heat the oven to 375 degrees F. Pat the fillets gently with a paper towel and place each one on a piece of aluminum foil large enough to fold over and completely cover the fish. Drizzle each fish with lemon juice and season with salt and pepper. Scatter some garlic slices over the

6	walleye fillets (about 8 ounces each), fresh or frozen and thawed
	Juice of 3 lemons
	Salt and freshly ground black pepper
1	large clove garlic, thinly sliced
3	tablespoons butter

fish. Cut the butter into 6 equal pieces and place one on top of each fillet. Fold the foil over the fish, crimping the edges to make secure packets, and place on a baking sheet. Bake for 30 minutes, or until the fish flakes easily with a fork. Turn the fish out of the packets onto plates and serve immediately or, for a more casual campfire supper, serve right in the foil.

SERVES 6

TEN THOUSAND LAKES of MINNESOTA

MINNESOTA

The Land of Ten Thousand Lakes

MISSISSIPPI MUD CAKE

Some old family recipes for this tasty, rich dessert call for the addition of strong black coffee and bourbon. This version, sure to please kids of any age, is a traditional favorite for family get-togethers and holiday parties.

Heat the oven to 350 degrees F. Grease and flour a 9-by-13-inch baking pan. Melt the butter in a heavy saucepan over low heat. Add the cocoa and blend with a whisk until smooth. Remove from the heat and let cool slightly. Beat the sugar and eggs in a mixing bowl with an electric mixer until well blended, 3 to 4 minutes. Add the flour, butter-cocoa mixture, and vanilla and beat until smooth. Stir in the pecans. Pour the mixture into the prepared pan. Bake for 25 to 30 minutes, until a toothpick inserted in the

1	cup (2 sticks) butter
1/3	cup unsweetened cocoa powder
2	cups sugar
4	eggs
1 1/2	cups all-purpose flour
1	teaspoon vanilla extract
1	cup chopped pecans
1	jar (7 1/2 ounces) marshmallow creme

Mud Frosting

1/2	cup (1 stick) butter
1/3	cup unsweetened cocoa powder
4	cups powdered sugar
1/2	cup milk

COTTON PICKIN TIME!

center comes out clean and the top is crackly. While the cake is still very hot, spoon the marshmallow creme in dollops over the top, let it start to melt, and then smooth with a spatula. Let the cake sit for a few minutes while you prepare the frosting.

To prepare the Mud Frosting: Melt the butter in a heavy saucepan over low heat. Add the cocoa and blend with a whisk until smooth. Pour the mixture into a mixing bowl and gradually beat in the powdered sugar and milk with an electric mixer to form a smooth, thick icing. Spoon the frosting over the marshmallow layer in dollops and smooth it carefully with a spatula, concealing the marshmallow layer as much as possible. Let the cake cool completely and the frosting set before serving.

SERVES 12 TO 14

KANSAS CITY STRIP STEAK

In 1871, the Kansas City Stockyards were organized, and this part of the world became synonymous with beef. To cook a steak according to the tradition practiced in Kansas City for more than one hundred years, always use a grill and enjoy the meat medium-rare. And remember, never use a fork to turn the steaks, or the juices will run out—use tongs instead.

Prepare a charcoal fire or preheat a gas grill on high. Season the steaks with pepper and sear for 1 minute per side on the hot grill. Turn over to the first side and grill for 4 minutes. Turn the steaks and grill the opposite side for 3 minutes for medium-rare, or to desired doneness. When done, season with salt. Let the steaks rest for a minute or two before you cut into them.

SERVES 4

4	beef strip steaks or top sirloin steaks (10 to 14 ounces each) about 1 inch thick
	Freshly ground black pepper
	Salt

Note: In Kansas City, grilling is done as much by touch as by time. To learn this technique, discover the different textures of your hand. Using the first finger and thumb from your right hand, feel the fleshy web between the first finger and thumb of the left hand. If you begin closest to the palm, it feels firm—that is what a well-done steak should feel like when you press on the center. Move halfway out to the softest part of the web—that is what a medium steak should feel like when you press on the center. Lastly, feel the very fleshy, soft part of the web—that is how a rare steak should feel when you press on the center.

GUEST of MISSOURI

Invited By
MISSOURI DIVISION
of
RESOURCES and DEVELOPMENT

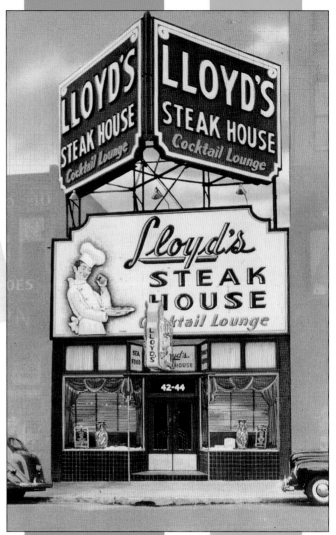

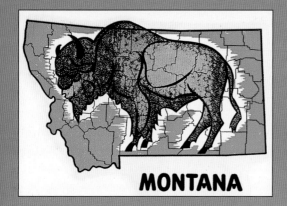

MONTANA

BUTTE PASTIES

Montana has a rich mining history, which has given the state its nickname. Although gold was discovered in Butte around 1854 and silver soon after, by 1898 mines around the town already supplied more than 40 percent of the world's copper. These meat pies were popular in the lunch pails carried by English and Irish miners.

Heat the oven to 350 degrees F. Divide the pastry into two equal pieces and on a lightly floured surface, roll each piece out into a rectangle approximately 18 inches by 8 inches. Cut each piece crosswise into three equal, smaller rectangles. Arrange equal amounts of carrots, onions, potatoes, and meat over the center of the rectangles and drizzle each with a few spoonfuls of gravy. Season with salt and pepper. Fold the short ends of the pastry up over the filling and crimp the top and side edges to seal tightly. Poke the

	Unbaked pastry for a 2-crust pie
2	medium carrots, peeled and thinly sliced
3	medium onions, chopped
6	medium potatoes (about 2 pounds), peeled and thinly sliced
1 1/2	pounds beef flank steak, thinly sliced crosswise
1	cup homemade or canned beef gravy
	Salt and freshly ground black pepper

tops in several places with a fork and use a spatula to carefully slide the pasties onto a baking sheet. Bake for 45 to 60 minutes, until lightly browned. Serve warm. Refrigerate any cooled leftover pasties and use them within two days.

SERVES 6

COME ON IN, STRANGER!

GLAD T' SEE YOU.

1937
MONTANA
HIGHWAY MAP

PUBLISHED BY
STATE HIGHWAY COMMISSION
FOR FREE DISTRIBUTION

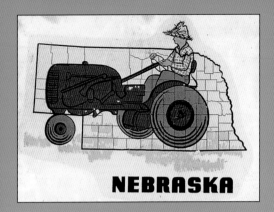

NEBRASKA

SOUR CREAM COFFEE BREAD

After World War II, Nebraska's wheat producers were instrumental in establishing a strong export market for their grain surplus, as well as promoting baking statewide. Baking contests have long been popular events. Here's a recipe adapted from a recent blue-ribbon winner at the Nebraska State Fair.

Heat the oven to 350 degrees F. Grease a 10-inch tube pan. Combine 1/2 cup of the sugar, the nuts, and the cinnamon in a small bowl and set aside. Combine the flour, baking powder, and baking soda in a bowl and blend with a whisk until combined. Set aside. Beat the remaining 1/2 cup sugar and the butter in a mixing bowl with an electric mixer until light. Add the eggs and vanilla and beat until smooth, about 3 minutes.

1	cup sugar
1	cup chopped walnuts or pecans
1	teaspoon ground cinnamon
2	cups all-purpose flour
1	teaspoon baking powder
1	teaspoon baking soda
1/2	cup (1 stick) unsalted butter
2	eggs
1	teaspoon vanilla extract
1	cup sour cream

Topping

2	tablespoons butter
1	cup powdered sugar
2	tablespoons milk
1/2	cup chopped walnuts

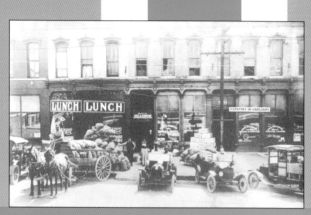

Add the flour mixture and sour cream and beat for about 3 minutes, until smooth. Spread half of the batter into the prepared pan. Sprinkle with the sugar and nut mixture. Top with the remaining batter. Bake 45 to 50 minutes, or until the cake springs back when lightly touched and it is just starting to pull away from the sides of the pan. Let the cake cool in the pan on a rack for 10 minutes before inverting it out of the pan to cool completely.

To make the topping: Melt the butter in a medium saucepan over low heat. Stir in the powdered sugar and milk until smooth. Remove from the heat, stir in the walnuts, and spoon over the top of the cooled cake, letting it run down the sides.

SERVES 8 TO 10

OUTDOOR NEBRASKA

OFFICIAL MAP

COMPLIMENTS OF

GAME FORESTATION AND PARKS COMMISSION

STATE OF NEBRASKA

RENO RED

Each year, the World's Championship Chili Cookoff is held in Reno, and residents throughout Nevada are serious about what constitutes a proper effort. This recipe, which uses beer, vinegar, and stewed tomatoes, is based on the city's namesake version that won the title in 1979. Be careful not to stir too vigorously, or it will turn mushy.

Put the chili peppers in a saucepan, cover with water, and bring to a boil. Reduce the heat to low and simmer for 30 minutes, or until the chilies are soft. Drain and set aside. Combine the beer and oregano in a small bowl and set aside. Meanwhile, divide the meat into three batches. Brown each batch in 1 tablespoon of oil in a heavy Dutch oven over medium heat, for about 5 minutes per batch, sprinkling generously with

6	dried red chili peppers (or to taste)
1/2	cup beer, at room temperature
1	tablespoon dried oregano
6	pounds coarsely ground beef chuck
3	tablespoons cooking oil
	Freshly ground black pepper
3	tablespoons chili powder
2	medium onions, chopped
6	cloves garlic, chopped
2	tablespoons cider vinegar
3	cups beef stock
1	can (4 ounces) diced green chilies
1	can (14.5 ounces) stewed tomatoes
2	teaspoons Tabasco sauce
	Salt

black pepper as it cooks. Drain each batch when browned and set aside. Return all the meat to the pot and add the chili powder, onions, and garlic. Stir to blend. Add about 1/4 cup of water and cook over low heat for about 15 minutes, stirring occasionally. Pat the drained chili peppers dry, slice open lengthwise with a sharp knife, and remove the seeds. Scrape out the pulp, and add it to the meat. Discard the skins. Hold a strainer over the meat and pour in just the beer, discarding the oregano. Add the vinegar, beef stock, green chilies, stewed tomatoes, and Tabasco sauce. Simmer 30 to 45 minutes, gently stirring now and then, until the flavors are well blended and the chili is piping hot. Season to taste with salt and pepper. Leftover chili keeps very well for several months in a tightly sealed container in the freezer.

SERVES 6 TO 8

Note: To make a very thick chili—the kind a spoon will stand up in—add only 2 cups of the beef stock after the beer. After 30 minutes, dissolve 2 tablespoons of corn flour (masa harina) in the remaining 1 cup of stock, add to the chili, and simmer for an additional 30 minutes, stirring frequently, until thickened.

APPLE CRISP

McIntosh, Cortland, Russett, Spartan, and dozens of other apple varieties are grown in orchards throughout New Hampshire. They were initially prized by colonial settlers as much for their ability to keep in root cellars through the winter as for their wonderful flavors. This old-fashioned dessert, a fall favorite, is especially good served warm with a scoop of vanilla ice cream.

Heat the oven to 350 degrees F. Grease a 9-by-13-inch baking dish. Peel, core, and slice the apples and place in a mixing bowl. Add the sugar and lemon juice and toss well. Spoon into the prepared baking dish.

5 to 6 firm medium apples (about 1 1/2 pounds)

1/2 cup sugar

Juice of 1/2 lemon

Topping

1 cup all-purpose flour

2/3 cup packed brown sugar

1/2 cup rolled oats

1 teaspoon ground cinnamon

1/4 teaspoon salt

1/2 cup (1 stick) chilled unsalted butter, cut into pieces

NEW
HAMPSHIRE

To make the topping: Combine the flour, brown sugar, oats, cinnamon, and salt in a food processor and pulse until smooth. Add the butter and pulse for several seconds, just until the mixture looks like damp crumbs. Crumble the topping over the apples. Bake for 30 minutes, or until the topping is golden and you can see juice bubbling in the pan. Let cool slightly before serving.

SERVES 8 TO 10

NEW HAMPSHIRE

Land of Scenic Splendor

Printed in New Hampshire

SALTWATER TAFFY

Soon after the Atlantic City Boardwalk was built in 1870, enterprising merchants in the area sold boxes of taffy candy to tourists who promenaded along the ocean. This souvenir confection has been popular along the Jersey Shore ever since, and is still made today in countless flavors.

Combine the water and salt in a heavy saucepan. Stir in the sugar, cornstarch, and corn syrup and cook over medium heat, stirring constantly, until the mixture comes to a boil and the sugar dissolves, about 3 minutes. Stop stirring, and continue cooking for 10 to 15 minutes, until the mixture reaches 265 degrees F on a candy thermometer, or when a small amount forms a firm but not hard ball when dropped in a glass of cold water. Stir in the butter and pour the hot

3/4	cup warm water
1	teaspoon salt
1	cup sugar
2	tablespoons cornstarch
1/2	cup light corn syrup
2	tablespoons butter, plus more for hands
1	teaspoon flavored extract (see Note) such as peppermint or vanilla
	powdered sugar for dusting

syrup onto a greased cookie sheet. Sprinkle the extract over the poured candy syrup. With a spatula or candy scraper, begin working the hot syrup by scraping it toward the center of the cookie sheet, getting under it, lifting and turning the mixture until it is cool enough to handle.

Grease your hands with butter or vegetable oil and begin pulling it up with your fingers into a length no more than 18 to 20 inches. Keep folding it back on itself and pulling out again. The taffy will be very sticky at first, but as you work it for about 10 minutes it will become opaque and firm. When ridges form as you pull, gather the taffy together, pull out several ropes about 12 to 14 inches long, and let them fall on a clean surface that is lightly dusted with powdered sugar. Cut the ropes into 2-inch pieces, and wrap each piece in a square of wax paper. Store in an airtight container for up to 3 weeks.

MAKES ABOUT 1 DOZEN PIECES

Note: You can flavor taffy with flavored extracts such as anise, lemon, orange, peppermint, and wintergreen. Look for extracts in large supermarkets or purchase them online from baking supply companies.

SANTA FE CHICKEN

This zippy method of preparing chicken has appeared on local menus since the 1940s. It always uses a marinade, and is especially good cold, served as a salad. The following recipe was a 1989 winner at the National Chicken Cooking Contest. Serve with corn, hot rolls, and an avocado salad.

Combine all the marinade ingredients in a medium bowl. Place the chicken between two pieces of wax paper and gently pound until 1/4 inch thick. Arrange the chicken in a single layer in a large plastic zip-lock bag. Add the marinade, close the bag, and marinate in the refrigerator, turning once, for at least 1 hour and up to 24 hours.

continued

Marinade

1/4	cup olive oil
	Juice and zest of 1 small lime
1	clove garlic, crushed
1	ounce tequila
1/4	teaspoon bottled hot pepper sauce
1/8	teaspoon liquid smoke flavoring
1/4	teaspoon salt
2	whole chicken breasts (about 8 ounces each) halved, boned, and skinned
2	sweet red bell peppers
1/4	cup jalapeño jelly

NEW MEXICO
STATE HIGHWAY DEPT.

SANTA FE N.M.

NEW
MEXICO

THE
SUNSHINE STATE

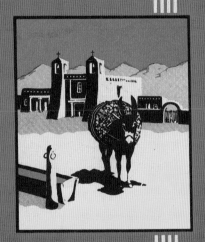

SHOWING
U.S. HIGHWAYS

OFFICIAL
ROAD MAP

MOTOR
PATROLLED

1935

PRINCIPAL
STATE ROADS

FOR
FREE DISTRIBUTION

To roast the bell peppers, place them under the broiler and turn often until charred. Cool. With the point of a sharp knife, remove stem, seeds, and skin. Cut into 8 strips and reserve. Heat the broiler. Remove the chicken from the marinade and place on a broiler pan; brush liberally with the marinade. Arrange the oven rack so the chicken is 6 inches from the heat and broil about 8 minutes, until browned. Turn and broil 8 minutes more or until the chicken is brown and a

fork can be inserted with ease. While the chicken is cooking, melt the jelly in a small saucepan over low heat. Brush the cooked chicken with some of the melted jelly. Place 2 roasted bell pepper strips to form an X on each breast half; spoon on remaining jelly. Return the chicken to the oven and broil until brown and slightly glazed, about 4 to 5 minutes longer.

SERVES 4

"The Land of Enchantment"

OFFICIAL 1938

ROAD MAP of NEW MEXICO

Welcome to NEW MEXICO

PREPARED FOR FREE DISTRIBUTION BY THE
NEW MEXICO STATE HIGHWAY DEPARTMENT
SANTA FE, NEW MEXICO

SHOWING U.S. HIGHWAYS
AND PRINCIPAL STATE ROADS
Motor Patrolled

CHEESECAKE

New Yorkers take their cheesecake seriously. Among the most beloved purveyors have been Lindy's, a deli at Broadway and 51st Street started by Leo Linderman in 1921 (it closed in 1969), and Juniors, a Brooklyn landmark founded by Harry Rosen in 1950 and still going strong. Although homemade cheesecake never tastes quite like the restaurant version, this one will give you a good taste of the real thing. To dress it up, top with cherry pie filling or whole-berry cranberry sauce.

continued

Crust

1/4 **cup (1/2 stick) butter, melted**

1 **cup (about 6) crushed graham cracker crumbs**

1/4 **cup walnuts or pecans, finely ground**

Filling

3 **packages (8 ounces each) cream cheese, at room temperature**

1 **cup sugar**

3 **eggs**

1/2 **cup sour cream**

1 **teaspoon vanilla extract**

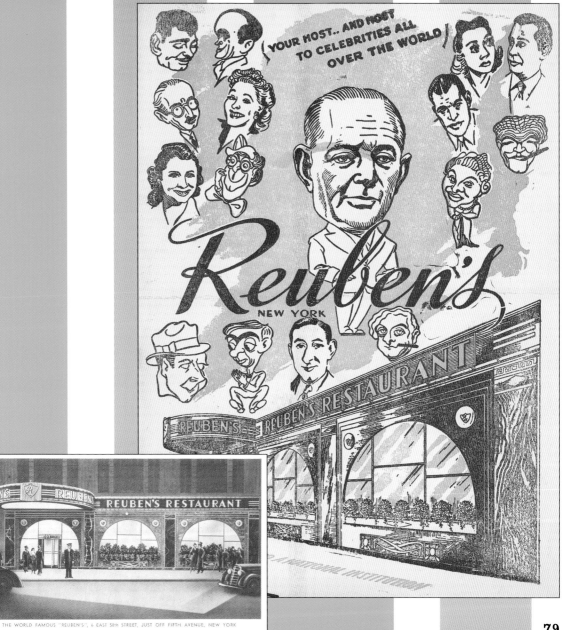

YOUR HOST.. AND HOST TO CELEBRITIES ALL OVER THE WORLD

Reuben's
NEW YORK

REUBEN'S RESTAURANT

THE WORLD FAMOUS "REUBEN'S", 6 EAST 58th STREET, JUST OFF FIFTH AVENUE, NEW YORK

Heat the oven to 325 degrees F. Generously grease the bottom and sides of a 9-inch springform pan. To make the crust: Melt the butter in a small saucepan over low heat; remove from heat. Add the graham cracker crumbs and nuts and stir until mixed. Press the damp crumbs evenly into the bottom of the prepared pan. Set aside.

To make the filling: With a hand-held or standing electric mixer, beat the cream cheese in a large mixing bowl until soft. Gradually add the sugar alternately with the eggs, beating on low speed just until smooth. Add the sour cream and vanilla and gently mix until smooth. Pour the filling over crust and smooth the top with a spatula. Place the pan on the middle rack of the oven. Set a large, flat baking dish containing 1 inch of water on the rack underneath the cheesecake. Bake for 45 minutes (don't peek), or until set in the middle. Turn off the heat but leave the cake in the oven for 20 minutes longer. Remove to a rack and let it cool completely. Cover with plastic wrap and chill overnight before serving.

SERVES 8 TO 10

A GUIDE *to and from*
NEW YORK

A GUIDE *to and from*
NEW YORK

BALTIMORE & OHIO
TRAIN CONNECTION

LIBERTY ST. ROUTE

049·030

BALTIMORE & OHIO R R

FROM THE TRAINSIDE TO THE METROPOLIS VIA MOTOR COACH

SWEET POTATO CASSEROLE

From the colonial era through the mid-1940s, just about every farm in North Carolina had its own sweet potato patch. Although per-person annual consumption in the United States. has dropped from thirty-one pounds in 1920 to below four pounds today, North Carolina continues to lead the nation in sweet potato production, and in 1993 the tuber was named the official state vegetable. Here's an especially popular local recipe. Serve with ham and baked apples.

3   cups cooked, mashed sweet potatoes (about 2 pounds sweet potatoes)

1   cup sugar

2   eggs

1   teaspoon vanilla

1/2   cup (1 stick) butter, at room temperature

Topping

1/3   cup butter

1   cup packed brown sugar

1/2   cup all-purpose flour

1   cup chopped nuts

Heat the oven to 350 degrees F. Grease a 1 1/2 quart casserole dish. In a mixing bowl combine the sweet potatoes, sugar, eggs, vanilla, and butter until smooth. Transfer the mixture to the baking dish.

To make the topping: Melt the butter over low heat in a medium saucepan. Stir in the brown sugar and cook for a minute or two, until the sugar dissolves. Mix in the flour and the nuts. Sprinkle the mixture evenly over the casserole. Bake for 30 minutes, until the top is slightly crusty and the mixture is piping hot.

SERVES 6 TO 8

Color Parade

in NORTH CAROLINA

DAKOTA BREAD

From 1905 to 1920, North Dakota's population more than tripled with the arrival of immigrants from Scandinavia and Germany. Many became the thrifty, hardworking farmers who weathered the Depression and prospered with the wartime economy. Today, North Dakota farmers grow more than 50 percent of the high-protein spring wheat produced in the United States—which yields a flour beloved by bread bakers for the structure and elasticity it gives to yeast doughs.

In a small bowl, sprinkle the yeast in the warm water and stir to dissolve. In a large bowl, mix the oil, egg, cottage cheese, honey, and salt until well combined. Add the dissolved yeast and 2 cups of the bread flour, beating with a

1	package (1/4 ounce) active dry yeast
1/2	cup warm water (105 degrees to 115 degrees F)
2	tablespoons sunflower or vegetable oil
1	egg, plus 1 egg white, beaten, for brushing
1/2	cup cottage cheese
1/4	cup honey
1	teaspoon salt
2	to 2 1/2 cups bread flour
1/2	cup whole-wheat flour
1/4	cup wheat germ, plus 1 tablespoon for sprinkling
1/4	cup rye flour
1/4	cup rolled oats
	Cornmeal for pan

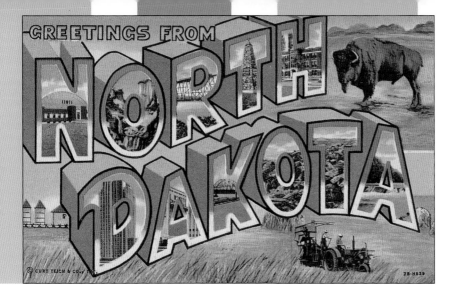

large wooden spoon until the flour is moistened. Gradually stir in the whole-wheat flour, 1/4 cup wheat germ, the rye flour, and rolled oats, plus enough of the remaining 1/2 cup bread flour to make a soft, slightly sticky dough.

On a floured surface knead the dough for about 10 minutes, or until it is smooth and elastic. Place the dough in a greased bowl and cover loosely with oiled plastic wrap. Let rise in a warm place until doubled in size, about 30 minutes. Punch down the dough. Shape into one round loaf. Place in a greased pie pan sprinkled with cornmeal. Cover with oiled plastic wrap and let rise until doubled in size, about 1 hour.

Heat the oven to 350 degrees F. Brush the bread with the beaten egg white. Sprinkle with the 1 tablespoon wheat germ. Bake for 35 to 40 minutes, or until the bread sounds hollow when you tap it gently with your knuckles.

MAKES 1 LOAF

OHIO

BUCKEYE
STATE

The Buckeye State

BUCKEYE BALLS

Ohio gets its nickname from the buckeye trees that once covered its hillsides, but the term has a political connotation, too. In the presidential campaign of 1840, when William Henry Harrison's opponents tried to insult him by calling him "the log cabin candidate," he turned to the buckeye to emphasize his rural roots, and used a buckeye cabin and strings of the tree's nuts as campaign emblems. This candy is easy enough for kids to make, and has long been popular at bake sales and county fairs.

¹/₂ **cup (1 stick) butter, melted**

3 ¹/₂ **cups powdered sugar**

2   **cups creamy peanut butter**

1   **teaspoon vanilla extract**

2   **cups (12 ounces) semisweet chocolate chips**

1   **tablespoon solid vegetable shortening (optional)**

Combine the melted butter, powdered sugar, peanut butter, and vanilla in a large bowl and stir until well blended and smooth. Chill for 2 hours, or until firm enough to easily handle. Roll the mixture into 1-inch balls and place on a sheet of wax paper. Melt the chocolate chips

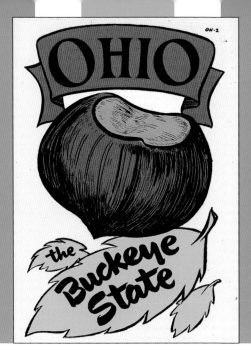

and shortening, if using, in the top of a double boiler over simmering water, stirring until smooth. (The shortening makes the chocolate shiny.) With a thin skewer or a toothpick, spear each ball and dip it into the melted chocolate, leaving a small area uncovered to make it look like a buckeye nut. Place the dipped balls back on the wax paper to cool and remove the toothpicks. Drip a bit of melted chocolate over the holes made by the toothpicks. Chill until firm. Store in an airtight container in the refrigerator for up to 4 weeks.

MAKES 18 TO 24

OKLAHOMA

CHEROKEE TULSA WILL ROGERS MEM.

OKLAHOMA CITY

FORT SILL KIAMICHI MTS

Everything's goin' OKAY

CHICKEN-FRIED STEAK

In 1988, the Oklahoma state legislature approved the "Official State Meal," which included this classic beef dish, which does taste surprisingly like chicken. You may use one round steak instead of the four cutlets if you prefer, but be sure to give it a good pounding with a meat tenderizer before using it in the recipe. The meat mustn't be tough. Serve with mashed potatoes and green beans.

1	**cup all-purpose flour**
1/2	**teaspoon salt**
1/2	**teaspoon freshly ground black pepper**
1/2	**teaspoon paprika**
1/2	**teaspoon dry mustard**
1	**egg**
1	**cup milk or buttermilk**
	Vegetable oil for frying
4	**beef cube steaks, about 6 to 8 ounces each and 1/2 inch thick, or one 2-pound boneless beef round steak, about 1/4 inch thick before tenderizing**

Beverly Osborne and his Chicken in the Rough Western girls going to the FFA and 4-H Club Live Stock Auction. It is the custom at Beverly's to buy a champion each year.

Combine the flour, salt, pepper, paprika, and mustard in a shallow dish. Beat the egg with the milk in a second shallow dish. Pour vegetable oil into a large skillet to a depth of about 1/2 inch and heat to 360 degrees F on a deep-frying thermometer. As the oil heats, dip each steak into the seasoned flour, shake off the excess, dip into the egg mixture, and then dip into the flour again, gently shaking off the excess flour a second time. Place the prepared steaks on a large platter. When the oil is hot, carefully drop in each steak. Cook for 4 to 5 minutes, until golden brown; turn carefully, and cook another 4 to 5 minutes, until golden brown. Drain on paper towels. Eat at once or keep warm in a 200 degree F oven until ready to serve.

SERVES 4

BLACKBERRY PIE

In 1927, the United States Department of Agriculture and Oregon State University's Experimental Station began a breeding program to cross domestic hybrid blackberry varieties, such as the boysenberry, loganberry, and youngberry, with ten native selections. In the decades since, their work has paid off. With its well-drained, fertile soil, gentle spring rains, and moderate summer weather, Oregon's Willamette Valley currently produces 85 percent of the U.S. blackberry crop and the state ranks as the nation's number one blackberry producer.

Unbaked pastry for a 2-crust, 9-inch pie, rolled into two 11-inch rounds

4	cups fresh blackberries
3/4	cup sugar
1/2	cup all-purpose flour
2	tablespoons milk

Heat the oven to 425 degrees F. Line a 9-inch pie pan with one of the pastry rounds. In a large bowl toss 3 1/2 cups of the berries with 1/2 cup of the sugar and the flour. Spoon the mixture into the unbaked pie shell. Spread the remaining 1/2 cup of berries on top of the sweetened berries. Cover with the top crust. Seal and crimp the edges. Brush the top crust with milk and sprinkle with the remaining 1/4 cup sugar. Bake for 15 minutes. Reduce the heat to 375 degrees F and bake for 20 to 25 minutes longer, or until nicely browned.

SERVES 6 TO 8

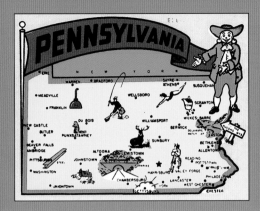

SHOOFLY PIE

Known for their traditional dress, horses and buggies, and pin-neat farms, the Pennsylvania Dutch, who live in Lancaster and surrounding Pennsylvania counties, are primarily of German descent and include the oldest group of Amish in the United States. Their culinary traditions include a long list of made-from-scratch dishes, including this ever popular, very sweet dessert.

Heat the oven to 400 degrees F. Line a 9-inch pie pan with the pastry. To make the crumbs: In a medium bowl combine the flour with the granulated and brown sugars. Using two knives or a pastry blender, cut in the butter until coarse crumbs form. Set aside.

Unbaked pastry for one 9-inch pie, rolled into an 11-inch round

Crumbs
- 1 1/2   **cups all-purpose flour**
- 1/2   **cup granulated sugar**
- 1/2   **cup packed brown sugar**
- 1/2   **cup (1 stick) chilled butter**

Filling
- 1/2   **cup unsulphured molasses**
- 3/4   **cup warm water**
- 1   **egg**
- 1   **teaspoon baking soda**

To make the filling: Combine the molasses and water in a mixing bowl. With a hand-held electric mixer or a standing electric mixer, beat in the egg and baking soda at low speed until the mixture is smooth, about 3 minutes. Add half the crumb mixture and beat at low speed just until smooth. Pour the mixture into the pie shell. Sprinkle the remaining crumbs over the filling. Bake for 10 minutes. Reduce the heat to 375 degrees F and bake for 30 to 40 minutes longer, or until the filling is set. Cool completely before serving.

SERVES 8 TO 10

RHODE ISLAND

THE SMALLEST STATE IN THE UNION

JOHNNY CAKES

Popular at restaurants and featured at May Day celebrations throughout Rhode Island, these old-fashioned pancakes can be made with white or yellow cornmeal or, if it's available, with locally milled stone-ground meal sold at specialty food markets. Some recipes claim lineage going back three hundred fifty years to Roger Williams, who founded Rhode Island as a haven for religious freedom in 1636. Serve the pancakes buttered, with maple syrup.

1	cup cornmeal
1/4	teaspoon salt
1	teaspoon sugar
1	cup boiling water
1/4	to 1/2 cup milk

Combine the cornmeal, salt, and sugar in a bowl and blend with a whisk. Gradually add the cup of boiling water, stirring constantly, until the mixture thickens. Let sit for 5 minutes. Gradually add enough of the milk to make a very thin batter. Let sit for 5 minutes longer. Heat a greased skillet or griddle over medium heat until a drop of water sizzles on the surface. Drop the batter by tablespoons onto the hot surface and cook over medium heat for 4 to 5 minutes, or until the edges are set; flip and cook on the other side for 5 minutes, until nicely browned and firm.

MAKES ABOUT EIGHT 3-INCH PANCAKES

SALT WATER
RHODE ISLAND
FOR YOUR
VACATION

PULLED PORK

When you say "barbecue" in South Carolina, it means pork, never beef. With the traditional way of cooking it used in this recipe, the fat melts away from the meat and the tough tissues soften, so the pork can, in fact, be pulled apart by hand. Pile the meat on buns, top with cole slaw and enjoy sandwich-style at a family party or casual get-together.

3 medium onions, sliced

1 pork roast (about 4 pounds)

8 to 10 whole cloves

2 bottles (16 ounces each) barbecue sauce

Salt and freshly ground black pepper

Put half the onions in the bottom of a slow cooker or Dutch oven. Stud the pork roast with the cloves and set it on top of the onion layer. Scatter around the remaining onions and add enough water to the pot to cover the meat. Cover the slow cooker and cook on low heat for 8 hours, until the meat is very easy to pierce with a fork. If using a Dutch oven, bring the liquid just to a boil, reduce the heat to

medium-low, cover, and cook for 4 hours, checking periodically to be sure there is at least 4 inches of liquid in the pan; add more water as necessary.

When the meat can easily be pulled apart with a fork, remove the pork and let it cool. Meanwhile, clean out the pot the pork cooked in. When cool enough to handle, pull the meat apart with your fingers and return it to the slow cooker or Dutch oven along with the barbecue sauce. Season with salt and pepper to taste. Cover the slow cooker and cook on high for 1 hour, until the sauce is slightly thickened and the meat is piping hot. If using a Dutch oven, cover the oven, bring just to a simmer, reduce the heat to low, and cook for 30 minutes, until hot.

SERVES 8 TO 10

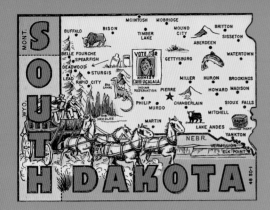

GRILLED STEAK

From the 1860s to the mid-1880s, herds of cattle roamed South Dakota's vast grasslands, and the cowboys who tended them left behind legends concerning life on the range. This recipe harks back to the days of the camp cook, but in truth, few real cowboys had an opportunity to dine on steak under the stars. This type of steak is more commonly found at South Dakota's modern-day guest ranches. Serve with fried potatoes, sautéed mushrooms, and a green salad.

1/4	cup black peppercorns
1	tablespoon chopped fresh cilantro
1	teaspoon salt
4	beef porterhouse steaks (about 8 ounces each)
1 1/2	cups red wine
1/4	cup bottled steak sauce
1/4	cup soy sauce
3	cloves garlic, crushed

Grind the peppercorns with a pepper mill into a small bowl. With a fork, mix in the cilantro and salt. Sprinkle both sides of the steaks with the mixture, pressing it into the meat. Arrange the steaks in a large glass baking dish. Combine the wine, steak sauce, soy sauce, and garlic in a small bowl and blend with a whisk. Reserve about 1/2 cup of the mixture for grilling and

"Albert"
WORLD'S LARGEST BULL

HIGHWAY MAP OF

SOUTH DAKOTA

1949

PUBLISHED BY
SOUTH DAKOTA STATE HIGHWAY COMMISSION
Governor George T. Mickelson, Chairman
Commissioners:
H. B. Test, Matt Stephenson, C. H. Gunderson
F. W. Mitchell, Secretary
H. C. Rempfer, Highway Engineer
A. H. Pankow, Publicity Director

TOURAIDE
CONOCO

SOUTH DAKOTA

pour the remainder over the steaks. Cover and refrigerate for at least 4 hours and up to 24 hours, turning once.

Prepare a charcoal fire or heat a gas grill to medium. Remove the steaks from the marinade; discard marinade. Place the steaks on the grill and cook to desired doneness, brushing them several times as they cook with the reserved 1/2 cup marinade. Allow about 5 minutes per side for medium. Let the steaks stand for a few minutes before slicing.

SERVES 4

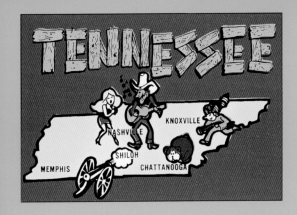

The Volunteer State

LYNCHBURG LEMONADE

Appalachian mountain people have a long and proud tradition of making corn whiskey in secret stills. In 1866, the clever Jack Daniels applied to the United States government for a permit to make whiskey, and his business in Lynchburg became the first licensed distillery in the country. Although the town is dry, this refreshing drink is popular locally, and throughout the United States.

Combine all ingredients in a cocktail shaker and serve over ice in a tall glass, or increase quantities and fill a punch bowl.

SERVES 1

1	ounce Tennessee whiskey, preferably Jack Daniels
1	ounce Triple Sec
1	ounce sweet and sour mix
2	to 4 ounces lemonade, Sprite, 7-Up, or lemon-lime soda

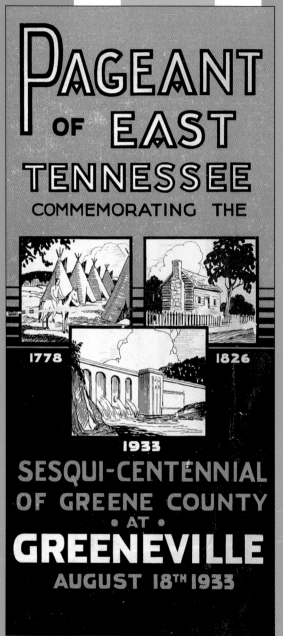

PAGEANT OF EAST TENNESSEE

COMMEMORATING THE

1778   1826

1933

SESQUI-CENTENNIAL OF GREENE COUNTY • AT • GREENEVILLE

AUGUST 18TH 1933

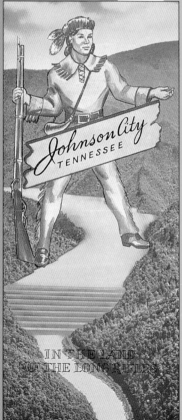

Johnson City
TENNESSEE

IN THE LAND
OF THE LONG RIFLES

BRAZOS RIVER CHILI

In 1977 the Texas Legislature made chili the official state dish. "A bowl of red" can be as hot as you wish; this version is quite mild, so add more chili peppers if you want it fiery. Purists in the state insist that chili mustn't contain beans, corn, or other such additions, regarding them as adulterations.

Heat the bacon drippings in a Dutch oven over medium-high heat. Dice the meat into 1/4-inch pieces, add to the Dutch oven, and brown on all sides, about 5 minutes. Remove to a platter with a slotted spoon. Add the garlic and onion to the pan and cook until soft, about 4 minutes. Return the meat to the pan, add the beef and chicken broths and tomato sauce, and bring

3	tablespoons bacon drippings
3	pounds beef top sirloin
4	large garlic cloves, minced
1	medium onion, finely chopped
3	cups beef broth
3	to 3 1/2 cups chicken broth
1	cup tomato sauce
2	teaspoons onion powder
1	teaspoon garlic powder
3	to 6 tablespoons chili powder
1	tablespoon Hungarian paprika
2	fresh jalapeño chilies, halved and seeded
1	teaspoon ground cumin
	Salt and freshly ground black pepper

just to a boil. Stir in 1 teaspoon of the onion powder, the garlic powder, 3 tablespoons of the chili powder, and the paprika. Float the jalapeño halves on the surface. Reduce the heat to low and simmer, covered, for 1 hour, until the mixture is slightly thickened and fragrant. (Check occasionally to be sure liquid covers the meat; if it looks dry, add a little bit more chicken broth.) Remove the jalapeños from the surface and stir in the cumin, plus the remaining teaspoon of onion powder and additional chili powder to taste. Put the jalapeños back on the surface, cover, and simmer over low heat for 1 more hour, until the flavors are well blended. Season to taste with salt and pepper. Serve hot.

SERVES 8 TO 10

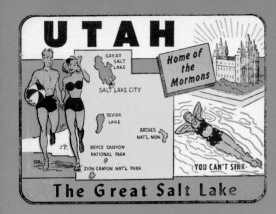

FUNERAL POTATOES

Despite its somber name and its association with Mormon funerals, this hearty casserole always turns up at church parties and school potlucks. The cheesy 1950s-style dish is so much a part of Utah culture it was represented by an official 2002 Olympic commemorative pin.

Peel the potatoes, cut into chunks, cover with water in a large kettle, and bring to a boil over high heat. Reduce the heat to medium and cook until soft, about 20 minutes. Drain the potatoes. Heat the oven to 325 degrees F. Grease a 9-by-13-inch baking dish. Combine the potatoes in a large bowl with the soups, sour cream, and green onions and mix well. Spread the mixture into the prepared pan. Sprinkle the cheese over the potatoes in an even layer.

9	to 10 medium boiling potatoes (about 3 pounds)
1	can (10 ounces) cream of celery soup
1	can (10 ounces) cream of chicken soup
2	cups sour cream
1	cup chopped green onions
2	cups (8 ounces) grated Cheddar cheese
2	cups corn flakes, crushed
2	tablespoons butter, melted

Toss the crushed corn flakes with the melted butter in a medium bowl and sprinkle over the top. Bake for 25 to 35 minutes, until bubbly.

SERVES 10 TO 12

UTAH
SIGHTS AND SCENES

UNION
PACIFIC
THE OVERLAND ROUTE
WORLD'S PICTORIAL LINE

For the Tourist

E. DICKINSON,
General Manager,

E. L. LOMAX,
Gen'l Pass'r and Ticket Agent,

OMAHA, NEB.

UTAH
-land of endless
scenic discovery

PAUL CLOWES

FLYING M
CAFE

CAFE   AIR CONDITIONED   DINING ROOM   CAFE

Gateway To

U.S. HIGHWAY 89 . . . Bryce Canyon . . . PANGUITCH, UTAH

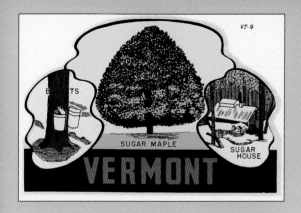

SUGAR ON SNOW

Vermont is the largest maple syrup producer in the United States, and for many generations Vermonters have passed along the secrets of tapping maple trees and boiling syrup. (It takes forty gallons of sap to make one gallon of syrup.) Sugar on Snow parties have long been popular springtime events. This sweet treat is traditionally served with pickles and doughnuts.

Heat the syrup and butter in a large kettle over medium-high heat, watching carefully. Reduce the heat if it threatens to boil over. When the syrup reaches 234 degrees F on a candy ther-

4	cups pure maple syrup
1/2	teaspoon butter
1	tub packed snow or well-crushed ice

mometer, remove from the heat and pour a spoonful of it over a small bowl of snow. If the syrup sits on top of the snow and clings to a fork like taffy, it's ready. Pack the snow or ice into individual bowls and pour the syrup over it in ribbons so it forms a lacy pattern over the top.

SERVES 8 TO 10

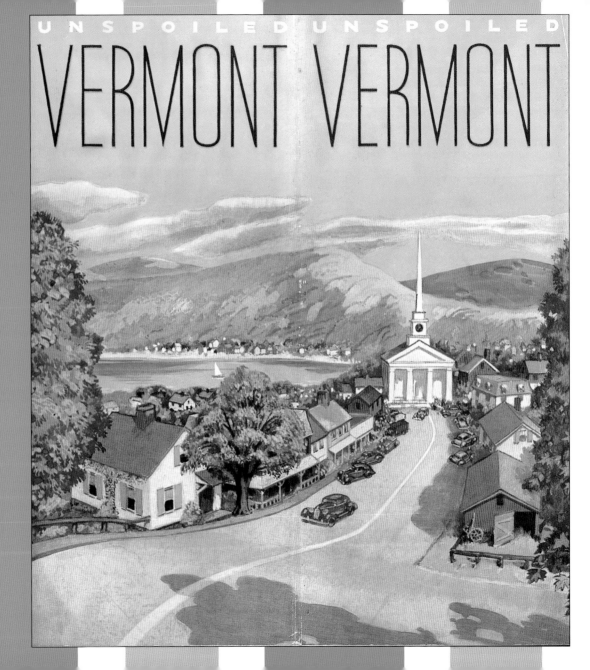

UNSPOILED VERMONT

The Old Dominion State

COUNTRY HAM

Hogs have been cured near Smithfield since the mid-1700s, and Virginians have a long, proud tradition of producing fine country hams. They're held so dear that the Barter Theater in Abingdon, founded in 1933 to allow Depression-poor residents to trade food for tickets, accepted "ham for Hamlet"—and still honors the custom, although today the trade would be in the theater's favor. Unlike modern, watered-down, and injected super-market hams, a true country ham is salt cured and slow smoked, with a haunting flavor that connects it to its past. Make the citrus glaze described in the recipe or use your favorite bottled glaze for extra flavor.

1	uncooked Virginia salt-cured ham (about 8 pounds)
1/2	cup packed brown sugar
1	tablespoon orange or lemon juice

Scrub the ham with a vegetable brush and warm water. Cut a thick slice off both ends and discard. Place the ham in a large kettle. Cover with cold water and soak for 12 to 24 hours at room temperature. Remove from the water and pat dry. Heat the oven to 325 degrees F. Place the ham fat-side up on a rack in a large roasting pan and pour water into the pan to a depth of about 2 inches. Bake about 2 1/2 hours (20 minutes per pound), basting frequently, until the

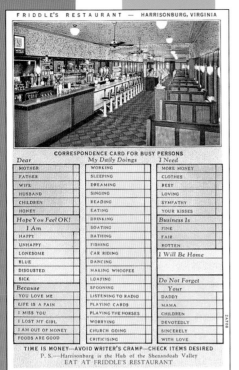

internal temperature reaches 155 degrees F. Remove the ham from the pan and trim off the skin and most of the fat.

To make the glaze, combine the brown sugar and orange juice in a small saucepan over medium heat. Bring to a boil, and cook for 2 minutes, stirring constantly, until the sugar melts. Spread a thin layer of glaze over the ham, return it to the oven, and bake for 20 to 30 minutes, or until the surface of the ham is brown.

SERVES 12 TO 14

APPLE DUMPLINGS WITH CARAMEL SAUCE

By 1826, settlers had discovered that the abundant sunshine and lava-rich soil in the eastern foothills of the Cascade Mountains created perfect apple-growing territory. But it wasn't until 1937 that the governor of Washington created a special commission to advertise apples, by law allocating one cent per box of fruit to go toward the marketing effort. It worked, and apples from Washington became known far and wide for their fresh flavors and crisp textures. Today, 70 percent of all apples grown in the United States come from Washington orchards.

Pastry

1 1/2	**cups all-purpose flour**
1/2	**teaspoon salt**
1/2	**cup (1 stick) chilled unsalted butter, cut into 1-inch pieces**
1/4	**cup cold water**
4	**medium apples, such as Jonagold or Cortland**
3	**tablespoons chilled unsalted butter**
3	**tablespoons packed brown sugar**
1	**teaspoon ground cardamom**

WASHINGTON

Sauce

    Peels and cores reserved from the 4 apples

1   **cup water**

    Juice of 1 lemon

1/2 **cup sugar**

To make the pastry: Combine the flour and salt in a food processor. Add the chilled butter and pulse the motor on and off several times. Add the water and pulse briefly, just until the mixture resembles crumbs. Dump the mixture out onto a piece of wax paper and gather it into a ball. Divide it into four equal pieces, and gently shape each piece into a flattened disc. Wrap in wax paper and chill for 30 minutes.

continued

To prepare the apples: With a sharp paring knife peel the apples and remove the cores, leaving the bottoms of the apples intact. (Reserve the peels and cores for the sauce.) In a small bowl using a pastry cutter, combine the butter, brown sugar, and cardamom until crumbly, and fill each cored apple with this mixture, dividing it equally.

On a lightly floured surface, roll each piece of chilled pastry dough into an 8-inch circle about 1/8 inch thick. Center each filled apple on a round of pastry dough; gather the dough and wrap it around the apples, leaving a small opening at the tops. (The apples can be wrapped and refrigerated for several hours or overnight before baking and serving.) About forty-five minutes before serving time, heat the oven to 350 degrees F and line a baking sheet with

parchment. Arrange the apples a few inches apart on the baking sheet and bake 35 to 40 minutes, or until the pastry is golden brown and the apple is fork tender.

To make the sauce: While the dumplings are cooking, put the reserved apple peels and cores in a small saucepan with the 1 cup water. Cook over medium heat for 15 minutes, or until very soft. Press the liquid through a strainer into a measuring cup. Return 1/2 cup of the strained liquid to the pan. Add the lemon juice and bring the liquid to a full boil over high heat. Add the sugar all at once and cook on high heat for 3 to 5 minutes, or until a small amount of the sauce holds its shape when dropped onto a chilled plate. Serve each apple hot or warm in a pool of the sauce.

SERVES 4

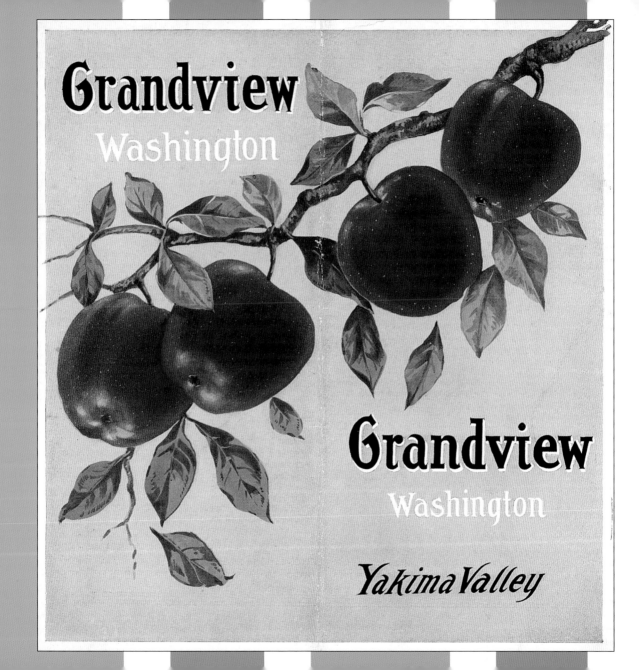

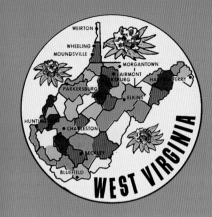

RAMPS AND POTATOES

Ramps, also known as wild leeks, emerge in early spring on north- and east-facing hillsides throughout West Virginia. They're prized by the locals for their strong flavor and are taken seriously as a spring tonic. For decades, Morgantown and Elkins, among many other towns, have celebrated them at springtime festivals. The oldest organized "ramp feed" is held in Richwood each year in late April.

Fry the bacon in a heavy skillet over medium heat for 5 minutes, until the edges are just starting to brown. Remove from the pan with a slotted spoon and reserve. Add the potatoes to the skillet and cook over medium heat for 10

1	**pound Canadian-style bacon, chopped**
4	**medium potatoes (about 1 1/4 pounds), peeled and diced**
1	**pound ramps, bulbs and leaves, finely chopped**
	Salt and freshly ground black pepper

minutes, turning frequently, until almost tender. Add the ramps and continue cooking for 5 minutes longer. Stir in the cooked bacon and heat through. Season with salt and pepper to taste. Serve hot.

SERVES 4 TO 6

114

WHO, WHAT, WHERE *In*

WEST VIRGINIA

Featuring The OFFICIAL 1947
WEST VIRGINIA HIGHWAY MAP

Scene of First Land Battle, Civil War, Philippi.

VISIT
WEST VIRGINIA SCENIC CROSSROADS
WEST VIRGINIA PUBLICITY COMMISSION

WEST VIRGINIA *Centennial*

1863 1963

SHEBOYGAN DOUBLE BRAT

German sausagemakers brought their craft to Wisconsin in the nineteenth century, and nowhere is a good sausage savored as it is in Sheboygan. Since 1959, the city has been the site of Bratwurst Day, held the first Saturday in August. All year long you'll find this tasty treat on the menu everywhere, from upscale restaurants to hamburger joints and mom-and-pop lunch counters. The ends of the brats should hang out of the bun a good 1/4 to 1/2 inch, providing an appetizing prelude to launch into the whole experience. And although nothing made outside the state tastes like a Wisconsin hard roll, in a pinch you can substitute bulkie-style deli rolls.

12	bratwurst
	Butter for rolls
6	Wisconsin hard rolls
	Coarse brown mustard for serving
1	to 2 Vidalia onions, sliced 1/8 inch thick
4	to 5 dill pickles, sliced like coins

Grill the brats slowly over the low heat of a hardwood charcoal fire or gas grill, turning occasionally, until cooked through, about 15 minutes. (According to Wisconsin timing standards, they need to cook for as long as it takes you to enjoy two beers.) Lightly butter the rolls, put two cooked brats in each, cover with mustard, and top with onion slices and pickle slices.

SERVES 6

While traveling in Wisconsin, **America's Dairyland,** and the Nation's all year Playground, on highway 41 and through the north limits of Fond du Lac, be sure to stop at **THE BEER HUT** for a brief rest and a fine lunch. You will find that Wisconsin Hospitality and our Services are unequalled.

Dobby's Bar and Cocktail Lounge, Middleton, Wisconsin

"Eau Claire is There!"

117

BUFFALO STEW

Before he founded his namesake town in Wyoming, Buffalo Bill Cody was said to have killed more than four thousand buffalo in eight months. This type of general slaughter made the American buffalo virtually extinct by 1900, but they have slowly made a comeback. From the thirteen left alive in Yellowstone Park, the herd there now numbers more than three thousand, and buffalo has been raised for meat throughout the West for the past fifty years. This heart-healthy meat, lower in cholesterol and calories than beef, has a rich taste.

2	pounds boneless buffalo meat, cut into cubes
	All-purpose flour, for dredging
2	tablespoons olive oil
2	cloves garlic, minced
2	medium onions, chopped
1	green bell pepper, seeded and chopped
1	can (14.5 ounces) diced tomatoes with their juice
1 1/2	cups beef stock or water
1/2	cup red wine
3	carrots, peeled and diced
4	potatoes, (about 1 1/4 pounds) peeled and cut into chunks
1/2	teaspoon dried marjoram
1/2	teaspoon dried thyme
	Salt and freshly ground black pepper

WYOMING

HOME ON
THE RANGE!

CASPER

the HUB OF WYOMING

Dredge the meat in flour and shake off excess. Heat the oil in a Dutch oven and brown the meat on all sides over medium heat. Remove from the pan and set aside. Add the garlic, onions, and bell pepper and sauté until soft, about 5 minutes. Add the tomatoes, stock, and wine, bring to a boil, and reduce the heat to a simmer. Add the browned meat, cover, and cook over low heat for 1 hour, until slightly thickened and fragrant. Add the carrots, potatoes, marjoram, and thyme and cook, covered, for 30 minutes longer, until the potatoes are soft. Season to taste with salt and pepper. Serve hot.

SERVES 6

RECIPE PERMISSIONS

California: Guacamole (page 22). Used by permission of California Avocado Commission.

Delaware: Baked Chicken (page 28). Used by permission of Delmarva Poultry Industry, Inc.

Hawaii: Sweet-and-Sour Spareribs (page 34). Used by permission of Hawaiian Electric Company, Inc.

Kansas: Pioneer Bread (page 44). Used by permission of Kansas Wheat Commission.

Kentucky: Mint Juleps (page 46). Used by permission of Call to the Derby Post, www.DerbyPost.com.

Maine: Steamed Lobster (page 50). Used by permission of Maine Lobster Promotion Council.

Michigan: Cherry Pie (page 56). Used by permission of Cherry Marketing Institute.

Missouri: Kansas City Strip Steak (page 62). Used by permission of Dan Cherrington, www.kansascitycooking.com.

New Mexico: Santa Fe Chicken (page 74). Used by permission of National Chicken Council.

North Dakota: Dakota Bread (page 84). Used by permission of North Dakota Wheat Commission.

Oregon: Blackberry Pie (page 90). Used by permission of Oregon Raspberry & Blackberry Commission.

Texas: Brazos River Chile (page 102). Used by permission of Patricia Mitchell, Texas Cooking Online, www.texascooking.com.

Vermont: Sugar on Snow (page 106). Used by permission of Vermont Maple Promotion Board.

Washington: Apple Dumplings with Caramel Sauce (page 110). Used by permission of Washington State Apple Commission.

Wisconsin: Sheboygan Double Brat (page 116). Used by permission of Michael S. Zeller, Johnsonville Sausage.

121

ILLUSTRATION CREDITS

Cover: Fred Harvey Food Map, linen postcard, 1943.

Front Flap: Travel sticker, ca. 1950.

1: *To And Through America by Pacific Mail and Southern Pacific Sunset Route,* ship booklet, 1914.

2: *Greatest Travel Bargain in History!,* Pullman train brochure, ca.1940.

3: Linen postcard, 1942.

5: *Greyhound Lines, Scenic Low-Cost Travel to All America,* bus brochure, ca. 1930s.

9: (left) *The Glorious 50,* state flags pamphlet published by State Mutual of America, ca. 1950; postcard produced in Italy, ca. 1910.

10: *Western Air Express,* brochure, 1929.

11: Travel sticker, ca. 1950s.

12: (left) *United States* road map published by American Automobile Association, ca. 1950s; (right) *Dinner is Served,* restaurant guide by Elizabeth E. Webber, editor, booklet cover, 1935.

13: *See the U.S.A. Missouri Pacific Way,* railroad brochure, 1928.

14: Travel decal, ca. 1950s.

15: (clockwise from top left) Real photo postcard, ca. 1910; travel decal, ca. 1950s; poster stamp, 1929.

16: Travel sticker, ca. 1940s.

17: *Alaska Tours,* booklet published by American Express Travel Service, 1935.

18: Travel sticker, 1938.

19: (clockwise from left) Arizona state road map, 1939; real photo postcard, 1943; linen postcard, 1951; travel decal line art, ca. 1950s.

20: Travel decal, ca. 1950s.

21: (clockwise from top left) Linen postcard, ca. 1940; travel decal, ca. 1950s; linen postcard, 1940.

22: (top) Travel decal, ca. 1950s; real photo postcard, ca. late 1940s.

23: *The Scenic Route to California: California via the Exposition Flyer,* railroad brochure, 1934.

24: Travel decal, ca. 1950s.

25: (clockwise from top left) Travel sticker, ca. 1940s; poster stamp, ca. 1930s; linen postcard, ca. late 1940s.

26: Travel decal, ca. 1950s.

27: (clockwise from left) Connecticut state road map, 1935; travel decal, ca. 1950s; Casino Grill oversized matchbook cover, ca. 1940.

28: Travel decal, ca. 1950s.

29: (clockwise from top left) Linen postcard, Salt Lake City, UT, ca. late 1940s; travel decal, ca. 1950s; die-cut menu, Daytona Beach, FL, ca. 1940.

30: Travel decal, ca. 1950s.

31: (left) Travel decal, ca. 1950s; travel brochure, ca. 1930.

32: Travel decal, ca. 1950s.

33: (left) Linen postcard, 1941; travel decal, ca. 1950s.

34: Travel decal, ca. 1950s.

35: (left) Travel sticker, ca. 1940s; travel booklet, ca. 1920s.

36: Travel decal, ca. 1950s.

37: (left) Linen postcard, 1948; travel booklet, ca. 1930.

38: Travel decal, ca. 1950s.

39: (clockwise from top left) Smooth linen postcard, ca. 1940; matchbook cover, ca. 1940s; travel decal, ca. 1950s.

40: Travel decal, ca. 1950s.

41: (clockwise from top) Linen postcard, ca. 1950; travel sticker, ca. 1950; matchbook cover art, ca. 1940s.

42: (top) Large letter linen postcard, ca. 1940s; Conoco travel decal, ca. 1940s.

43: (clockwise from left) Iowa state road map, 1954; travel decal, ca. 1950s; real photo postcard, ca. 1950.

44: Travel decal, ca. 1950s.

45: (left) Travel decal, ca. 1950s; travel sticker, ca. 1940s.

46: (top) Travel decal, ca. 1940; linen postcard, 1943.

47: (left) Large letter postcard, ca. 1940; *Kentucky Highways* travel booklet, ca. 1940.

48: Travel decal, ca. 1950s.

49: (left) "Harry Carpenter's Chicken in the Straw" postcard art, 1941; Louisiana state road map, 1939.

50: Travel decal, ca. 1950s.

51: (left) Linen postcard, ca. 1940; *Maine: Land of Smiling Skies*, travel booklet, 1929.

52: Poster stamp, ca. 1930s.

53: *Beautiful and Historic Frederick*, travel brochure, ca. 1930.

54: Travel decal, ca. 1950s.

55: (left) Travel decal, ca. 1950s; Pieroni's Sea Grills Menu, Boston, ca. 1930s.

56: Travel sticker, ca. 1940s.

57: (left) Real photo postcard, ca. late 1940s; *Vacation Land Michigan*, ca. 1930.

58: Travel sticker, ca. 1940.

59: *Minnesota: The Land of Ten Thousand Lakes*, travel booklet, ca. 1930.

60: Travel decal, ca. 1950s.

61: (left) Travel decal, ca. 1950s; *Natchez on the*

Mississippi: "Where The Old South Still Lives," travel brochure, 1975.

62: Travel decal, ca. 1950s.

63: (clockwise from top left) Travel sticker, ca. 1940; linen postcard, 1949; real photo postcard, ca. 1950.

64: Travel decal, ca. 1950s.

65: Montana state road map, 1937.

66: Travel decal, ca. 1950s.

67: (left) Real photo postcard, ca. 1910; *Outdoor Nebraska Official Map*, ca. 1940.

68: Travel decal, ca. 1950s.

69: (left) Harold's Club matchbook cover, ca. 1940s; *Nevada: Valley of Fire*, travel brochure, ca. 1950s.

70: Travel decal, ca. 1950s.

71: (left) Travel decal line art, ca. 1950s; *New Hampshire: Land of Scenic Splendor*, travel brochure, 1924.

72: Travel decal, ca. 1950s.

73: (left) Linen postcard, 1941; *Ocean City, New Jersey, Welcomes You*, travel booklet, ca. 1920s.

74: Travel sticker, ca. 1940s.

75: New Mexico state road map, 1935.

76: (left) Linen postcard, ca. 1940s; travel sticker, ca. 1950s.

77: New Mexico state road map, 1938.

78: Travel decal, ca. 1950s.

79: (left) Postcard, Hy Mariampolski Collection, ca. 1940s; Reuben's Menu, ca. 1950s.

80: Postcard, Hy Mariampolski Collection, ca. 1950s.

81: *A Guide to and from New York,* bus brochure issued by the B & O Railroad, ca. early 1930s.

82: Travel decal, ca. 1950s.

83: (left) Line art for travel decal, ca. 1950s; *Color Parade in North Carolina*, travel brochure, ca. 1950.

84: Travel decal, ca. 1950s.

85: (left) Large letter linen postcard, 1947; Conoco travel decal, ca. 1940s.

86: Travel decal, ca. 1950s.

87: (left) Travel decal, ca. 1950s; *Ohio Suggests an Auto Tour!*, travel booklet, ca. late 1940s.

88: Travel decal, ca. 1950s.

89: (clockwise from top left) Beverly's Steaks: Chicken in the Rough, chrome postcard, ca. 1950; map from back of Chicken in the Rough postcard; Rocky's Steak House, linen postcard, ca. 1950.

90: Travel decal, ca. 1950s; line art from travel decal, ca. 1950s.

91: Travel decal, ca. 1950s; *Oregon Primer,* travel booklet, 1911.

92: Travel decal, ca. 1950s.

93: (left) Linen postcard, ca. 1950; Pennsylvania state road map, ca. 1940s.

94: Travel decal, ca. 1950s.

95: Travel sticker, ca. 1940s.

96: Travel decal, ca. 1950s.

97: (left) County fair sticker, ca. 1940s; *Charleston Welcomes You,* travel booklet, ca. 1940.

98: Travel decal, ca. 1950s.

99: (clockwise from top left) chrome postcard, ca. 1960s; South Dakota state road map, 1949; Conoco travel decal, ca. 1940s.

100: Travel decal, ca. 1950s.

101: (clockwise from left) *Pageant of East Tennessee,* travel booklet, 1933; real photo postcard, Elk City, OK, ca. 1940; *Johnson City Tennessee,* travel brochure, ca. 1950.

102: Travel decal, ca. 1950s.

103: (left) chrome postcard, ca. 1960s; *To and Through Texas by Greyhound,* bus brochure, ca. 1930s.

104: Travel decal, ca. 1950s.

105: (clockwise from top left) *Utah Sights and Scenes for the Tourist,* railroad booklet, 1898; *Utah— Land of Endless Scenic Discovery,* travel booklet, 1939; Flying M Cafe, linen postcard, 1958.

106: Travel decal, ca. 1950s.

107: *Unspoiled Vermont,* travel booklet, ca. late 1930s.

108: Travel decal, ca. 1950s.

109: (clockwise from left) "Correspondence Card for Busy Persons," linen postcard, ca. 1940; smooth linen postcard, ca. 1940; travel decal, ca. 1950s.

110: Travel decal, ca. 1950s.

111: (left) Travel sticker, 1939; travel decal, ca. 1950s.

112: Travel decal, ca. 1950s.

113: *Grandview Washington,* travel booklet, 1911.

114: Travel decal, ca. 1950s.

115: (clockwise from left) West Virginia state road map, 1947; poster stamp, ca. 1930s; travel decal, 1963.

116: Travel decal, ca. 1950s.

117: (clockwise from top left) Linen postcard, ca. 1940s; travel decal, ca. 1950s; linen postcard, 1954; poster stamp, ca. 1915.

118: Travel decal, ca. 1950s.

119: (left) Travel decal, ca. 1950s; *Casper: the Hub of Wyoming,* ca. 1940.

121: Chromolith postcard, ca. 1910.

125: *Across America by Greyhound,* bus brochure, ca. 1940s.

Back flap: Travel sticker, ca. 1940s.

Back cover: (left) *To And Through America by Pacific Mail and Southern Pacific Sunset Route,* ship booklet, 1914; linen postcard, ca. 1940.

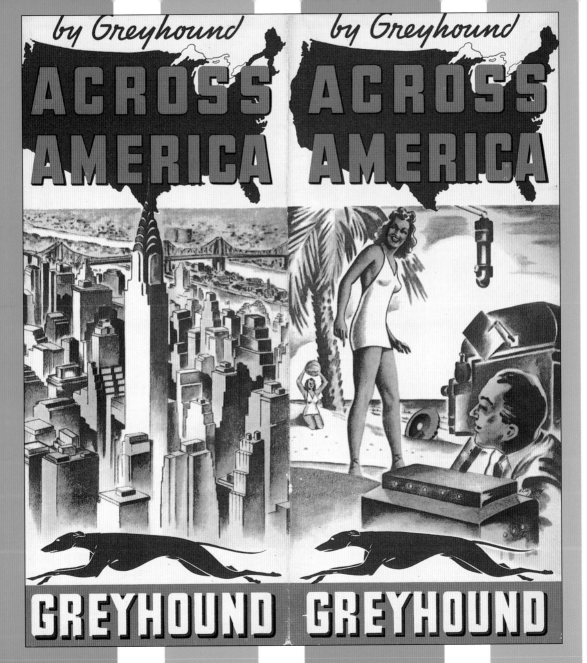

INDEX

TABLE OF EQUIVALENTS

The exact equivalents in the following tables have been rounded for convenience.

LIQUID/DRY MEASURES

U.S.	Metric
1/4 teaspoon	1.25 milliliters
1/2 teaspoon	2.5 milliliters
1 teaspoon	5 milliliters
1 tablespoon *(3 teaspoons)*	15 milliliters
1 fluid ounce *(2 tablespoons)*	30 milliliters
1/4 cup	60 milliliters
1/3 cup	80 milliliters
1/2 cup	120 milliliters
1 cup	240 milliliters
1 pint *(2 cups)*	480 milliliters
1 quart *(4 cups, 32 ounces)*	960 milliliters
1 gallon *(4 quarts)*	3.84 liters
1 ounce *(by weight)*	28 grams
1 pound	454 grams
2.2 pounds	1 kilogram

LENGTH

U.S.	Metric
1/8 inch	3 millimeters
1/4 inch	6 millimeters
1/2 inch	12 millimeters
1 inch	2.5 centimeters

OVEN TEMPERATURE

Fahrenheit	Celsius	Gas
250	120	1/2
275	140	1
300	150	2
325	160	3
350	180	4
375	190	5
400	200	6
425	220	7
450	230	8
475	240	9
500	260	10